The PHILIPPINES
America's Forgotten Friends

GEOFFREY BOCCA

The PHILIPPINES
America's Forgotten Friends

Parents' Magazine Press · New York

Each Background Book is concerned with the broad spectrum of people, places, and events affecting the national and international scene. Written simply and clearly, the books in the series will engage the minds and interests of people living in a world of great change.

To G. P.

Library of Congress Cataloging in Publication Data

Bocca, Geoffrey.
    The Philippines: America's forgotten friends.

    (Background book)
    Bibliography: p.
    SUMMARY: A history of the Philippines stressing its political development and its tragic struggle in World War II.
    1. Philippine Islands—History. 2. Philippine Islands—Politics and government. [1. Philippine Islands—History] I. Title.
DS668.B76   959.9   73-12287
ISBN 0-8193-0709-2;
ISBN 0-8193-0710-6 (lib. bdg.)

CONTENTS

INTRODUCTION

IF ANY OTHER nation had achieved what the Philippines
has achieved, performed the prodigies of wartime valor that
the Philippines has performed, suffered catastrophe with
equal fortitude, it would have boasted of its achievements
from the ramparts of the United Nations. But such is the
nature of the Filipino that he tends to believe only the bad
that is said of him, and though he burns inside with patriotism, he takes even the most sincere compliment with considerable surprise and profound skepticism.

The Filipino habit of self-denigration is so ingrained that
the outsider is obliged, reluctantly, to blame the Filipinos
themselves for the ignorance, and worse, disinterest, shown
by the rest of the world in one of the most brilliant, colorful,
and heroic nations of the world, a nation of poets and intel-

1

lectuals capable also of the heights of moral and military exaltation.

But the four horsemen of the Apocalypse ride the Philippines. Pestilence, war, famine, and death arrive on the scene so regularly that they have become expected, if unwelcome, guests. Catastrophe looms with every sunrise on this archipelago of more than seven thousand islands. They are impossible to count with precision. (Some sink under the ocean. New islands appear. A few blow themselves to bits.) Even the appearance of the islands on the map of the world is heavy and eerie with foreboding. The Philippines looks, for all the world, like the fossilized remains of the British Isles—bleached bones in seven thousand artifacts, discovered in some blue desert of water on the wrong side of the globe; Luzon preserved as what remains of Scotland; Mindanao is seen in the south as a chunk of southeast England; the island of Palawan resembles a sliver of Ireland from northeast to southwest; and the Sulu Archipelago, bits of Devon and Cornwall.

General Douglas MacArthur probably understood the Philippine temperament better than any other American. This may have stemmed from the fact that his father, General Arthur MacArthur, commanded the American forces that conquered the country at the beginning of the century, but more probably stemmed from some inner mystic feeling which could well have wedded such a man to such a country. In his speech to the Philippine Congress immediately after the liberation of the Philippines from the Japanese in 1945, he told of the sufferings he had witnessed and heard in the country, and added, "But there was one thing I did not see, one thing I did not hear. I never saw a tear, and I never heard a whimper." In two tingling sentences he captured the entire spirit and personality of the enormously diversified people, and gave definition to their incredible war effort.

The struggle of the Philippine people in World War II was heroic and utterly tragic. Out of a population of just 20 million, the Philippines lost a million dead—men, women, and children, but mostly their fighting youth. This loss was proportionately almost twice as great as that of France in World War I, generally accepted as the yardstick of twentieth-century bloodletting. Only the Soviet Union lost more, with 20 million dead out of a population of more than 200 million, and that nation is still emotionally prostrated by the losses. The United States lost a million men in the Civil War, the bloodiest war of its history, when the combined population of the North and the South was 37 million.

These statistics have passed largely unnoticed in the outside world. Some world almanacs—*Information Please* to name just one—in listing the dead of World War II, leave out the Philippines altogether. An *Atlas of American History* published in 1968 under the distinguished imprimaturs of Macmillan in the United States, and Weidenfeld and Nicolson in Britain, does not mention the Philippines even in its section, "The United States in the Pacific."

The Pacific war, generally, caused little damage to Allied countries—the Japanese advanced too rapidly for that. Ex-

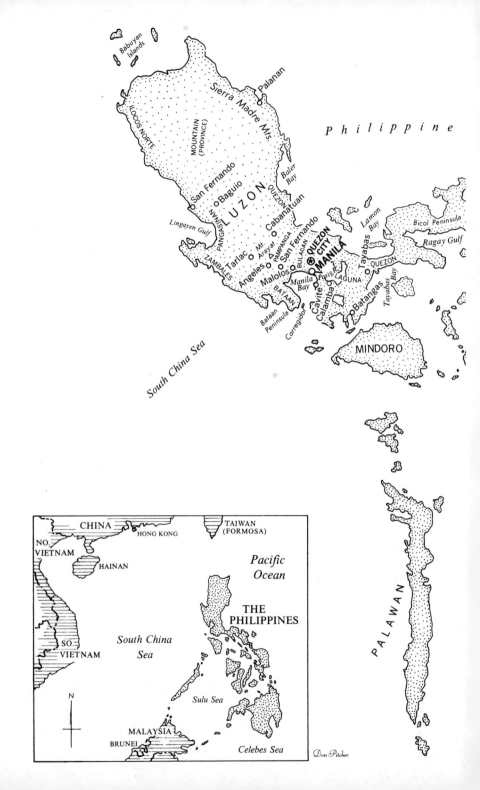

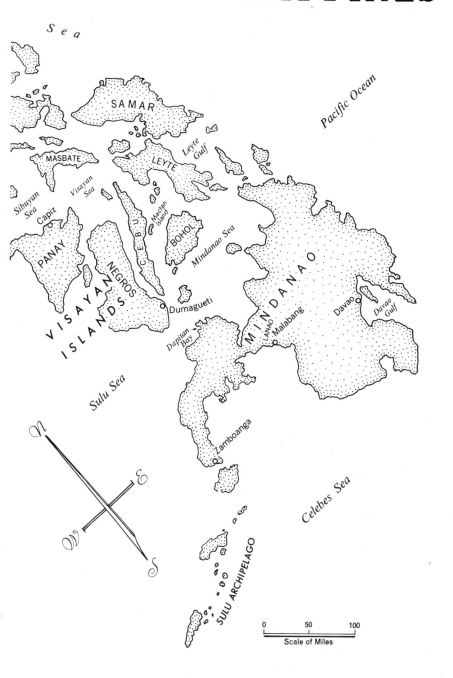

THE PHILIPPINES

Sea

SAMAR

MASBATE

Pacific Ocean

Leyte
Gulf

LEYTE

Sibuyan
Sea

Visayan
Sea

Capiz

Mactan
Island

CEBU

Mindanao Sea

PANAY

BOHOL

V I S A Y A N

NEGROS

I S L A N D S

Dumagueti

M I N D A N A O

Dapitan
Bay

Davao
Gulf

LANAO

Malabang

Davao

Sulu Sea

Zamboanga

Celebes Sea

SULU ARCHIPELAGO

0   50   100

Scale of Miles

cept in the Philippines where the people were savaged for five months at the beginning of the campaign, and where the Japanese made their last major stand. The city of Manila emerged from the war the most devastated city in the world, after Warsaw. But while the ravaged cities of Britain, Germany, and Poland have now been completely rebuilt, ugly gaps still scar central Manila, as well as other cities, such as Cebu and Baguio.

Here lies one of the many sources of modern Philippine schizophrenia: the awareness that while Europe was able to destroy itself and then almost casually make itself over again, the Philippines never seems to manage to get off its knees. Manila's terrifying crime rate is a hangover from the war that ended nearly thirty years ago.

The Filipino is a merciless self-critic. Because the country has not succeeded in mastering every one of its infinity of problems, Philippine newspapers, until they were suppressed by President Marcos in 1972, cried woe so deafeningly and so unflaggingly that one was sometimes surprised to look out of the window and find that the country was still there.

The Philippines has been called "a nation of survivors," in that every adult Filipino is alive today because he happened to avoid being killed, and every child is alive only because his parents escaped death. Of the Republic's six Presidents, four were war heroes. Inches are what every Filipino uses to measure his life. This is why the first thing every visitor to the Philippines notices is the youth of the people. Young men dominate government, business, banking, the press. There seem to be no old people.

The Filipinos are a people of astonishing maturity and sophistication, with a genius for living at peace with one another. While some countries are literally rent apart by merely two cultures—Canada, for example, and South Africa, and Northern Ireland, and Cyprus, and even Belgium—the Filipinos are divided by almost every known variety of race, creed, color, and religion, speaking 67 major dialects alone, as well as English, Spanish, and the official language, Tagalog.

They vary from the Moslems of Mindanao, fierce and unruly peoples to this day, to the Spanish-speaking high society of Manila, where the political salons are as witty and as lethal as any in Paris, to the naked Igorot tribes of the Mountain Province around Baguio. Almost the only people one does not find in the Philippines are the Jews. The Cebuano of Cebu, where Christianity was founded in Asia in 1665, is the Yankee trader of the Philippines. The Cebuano plans his life thriftily so that he can leave to each of his children as much as his father left to him. Capiz is Spanish, aristocratic, aloof. The largely middle-class population of Cavite, near Manila, has a quality of acquisitiveness that its neighbors do not always admire; these neighbors protest that the horse and cattle population of Cavite increases at a rate that defies all natural reproduction. The Ilocanos of Luzon are the fighters—"foot soldiers" as Gregorio Romulo has called them "in comparison with the Visayans who are instinctive cavalrymen."

Until 1972—a year that will recur whenever Philippine history is written—Philippine democracy was far advanced.

It was more mature in many ways than that in present-day France with its overtones of presidential paternalism and police brutality, or Italy, continually rent between the extremes of Fascism on the right and Communism on the left. It was much more experienced than democracy in Germany.

The author once had the educational experience of being received within the space of three weeks first by the late "Papa Doc" Duvalier, the tyrant of Haiti, and next by the then President Diosdado Macapagal of the Philippines. On the former occasion, one false twitch could well have resulted in death from a full dozen machine-guns posted at every window of the great reception hall of the Presidential Palace in Port au Prince. On the latter occasion, he was passed through by a casually uniformed sergeant at a desk, and within minutes was alone with the President. The difference in attitude typified both countries as they were then constituted.

Even before 1972 there ran, deep down in the Philippine consciousness, a sadness, as though it felt that its national destiny was to die. It is a shockingly insecure country. Despite its crime rate it is basically a country of exquisite gentleness, which emerges in all sorts of ways: in its charming cuisine; its folk dances; its invention of the *barong tagalog,* the national transparent shirt made out of pineapple fiber and beautifully embroidered; in the melodious language of Tagalog; and not least in its selection as its national hero of a man like José Rizal, of whom more will be said later. Nearly all nations like to identify themselves with their greatest war-

rior, and the Philippines has plenty of those, notably Andres
Bonifacio who fought the Spaniards almost single-handed,
armed with a bolo knife. But the nation prefers to identify
itself with Rizal, a poet, scholar, doctor, and humanitarian.

One of the few racial resentments that exist in the Philippines is directed against the oligarchic Spanish-speaking society leaders with their snobbish manners, almost un-
changed from the days of Spanish rule, which ended in
1898. Why this resentment exists will be explained in the
course of the book. The other Filipinos refer to these as "little
brown Spaniards." Consider this expression. The English
language, not to mention the French, German, and Russian,
is replete with short and hideous words of hate to describe
other races and colors; a society capable of no epithet more
beastly than "little brown Spaniards" is one deeply to be
cherished, so that no harm shall come to it.

But the Filipino is fatalistically aware that his destiny is
not in his hands. While for centuries Englishman clashed
with Pict, Scot, and Celt, while Europeans fought each
other in endless permutations of alliance and enmity, while
the American North fought the American South to a stand-
still, and Paleface fought Redskin to the death, the Filipinos
of all races lived reasonably in peace with one another,
never sought to destroy one another, and fought only outsiders seeking conquest. Which battles they invariably lost.

Chapter 1

A PEOPLE AT EASE

EVERY EVENING OVER Manila citizens and residents can witness one of the most spectacular free shows to be seen anywhere on earth or in heaven. As the sun goes down, white clouds assume fantastic forms against a sky that turns from cobalt blue to pink blood red. The sunset over Manila Bay is one of the glories of nature.

Coming as it does almost every evening for a lifetime, one may presume that it has burned deeply into the psyche of the native of Manila, this child of José Rizal, and one presumes correctly. In the Manilan personality the sunshine is almost visible. He is courteous, gentle, considerate to others. He smiles and laughs readily. Rudeness hurts him physically, like a blow.

An example of the generous, if fatalistic, Manilan temperament can be seen at rush hour. Traffic jams in Manila

10

are unique. For one thing, a Manilan driver stalled in a jam on a two-way street simply goes on the left side, followed by other equally brazen fellows, until the left side is as jammed as the right. Oncoming traffic, unable to move other than by ramming through, is quite likely to take to the sidewalk. But in this unspeakable uproar the outside visitor may notice something quite unusual. There is no yelling, no explosion of temper. The pretty, homebound secretaries, packed into the buses and the colorful jitneys— which are garishly painted and serve as something between a bus and a taxi—fan their moist brows and sigh in resignation. Car drivers sit back and turn on their car radios. Others spot friends and hail each other in English or Tagalog. They know that, in time, the traffic will move again, and tomorrow it will be the same thing all over again, and tomorrow is another day. So why allow anger to make one hotter than one is already.

Tagalog, a Malayo-Polynesian language, is mellifluous, soothing, and lends itself to poetry. Where the German language is dominated by the harsh "ch" sound, as in "ach," and Spanish is dominated by "th," the dominant sound in Tagalog is "ng." Even the murderous Huks, given their full name, emerge as the melodious Hukbong Mapagpagpalayang Bayan. Listening to Tagalog sometimes gives one the irreverent feeling that it was originally intended as a language for cats to understand. Here are the numbers one to ten in Tagalog: issa, talawa, tatlo, apat, lima, anim, pito, walo, siam and sampo, suggesting nothing so much as a large litter of Siamese kittens. The Philippine greeting of

"Mabuhay" is not so well known as the Hawaiian "Aloha," and only one word in Tagalog has broken into the American language: "bundocks," meaning "boondocks."

A lady visitor to Manila may very well be addressed as "Sir," and a man as "Madam." Tagalog has no sex, and some Philippine domestics find it confusing in English to differentiate between "he" and "she." The letters "p" and "f" are also frequently interchangeable and one must not be surprised if a smartly uniformed young officer describes himself as a "pighter filot." Growing up with three languages—English, Spanish, and one of the seventy Philippine languages—is a distinct problem for Philippine youths, and one that American educators have failed to solve despite the best of intentions. In the late 1960s, certain American educational interests began an ambitious campaign to teach Philippine children in the *barrios* (villages) the necessary languages by the use of cassettes.

"That is very interesting," said their Philippine colleagues, puzzled. "But where do we get the electricity?"

End of American experiment.

As always, throughout history, the Filipino finds deep joy in his religion, which is based on Spanish Catholicism, and faith is not far under the surface of even the toughest character. If President Marcos is to be believed, he consulted God before decreeing martial law, and the Almighty gave him the okay. Filipinos cannot do enough for Him. Cabinet officers and cynical business men take leaves of absence to attend *curcillos*—crash courses in faith renewal, in closed rooms from which day and night are excluded. The acceptance of that faith, so active and *involved,* results in curious and even revolting manifestations.

Every Good Friday, the citizens of every town and village may turn out to watch the flagellants. These are men, lightly masked, wearing loincloths and crowns of thorns, walking barefoot through the streets flogging themselves with chains until their own blood flows. Every hundred yards or so, they lie down on their faces while people wipe their feet on them.

The masks are worn to conceal their identities. It is said that many well-known men take part, making penances for their sins. At the end of the ordeal, the flagellants suck raw eggs to recover their strength. They then throw themselves into the Pasig River which, although polluted, is said to heal the scars they have inflicted on themselves. Only once has the author seen a flagellant remove his mask, ripping it off on the way to the Pasig and flinging it away. There was no sensitivity in the man's face. It was slashed, pockmarked, and evil, and he went away muttering to himself in a stream of prison curses in English and vernacular. Whatever degradation the man had endured in his lifetime, his spirit was still such that he was prepared to deliver this scourging to himself.

The Church and the press cluck indignantly at such a barbaric practice but do nothing to stop it, partly it is said, because the editors take part in the ordeal themselves, or if they do not, they damn well ought to. And on the same day, the press invariably reports, with photographs, stories of young

Filipinos in the *barrios* being nailed on the Cross and hung,
to share Christ's agony.

The Filipino is a voracious eater. He has a special cuisine
of his own, which he has borrowed from many sources—
American, Spanish, Indonesian, and Chinese. One of the
basic dishes is *adobo,* a garlic-flavored stew of fried pork and
chicken. *Sinigang,* frequently mentioned in the novels of
Rizal, is a kind of bouillabaisse. One particular delicacy is
bangus, which is sometimes called milk-fish, and resembles
the Mediterranean *loup de mer.*

The cuisine, however, can be elusive. One French gourmet
was so carried away by it that he bought a recipe book and
took it back with him to France. There, too late, he discovered that many of the best Philippine dishes ask for in-
gredients like swamp cabbage, Ceylon moss, mudfish, Hya-
cinth beans, and pith of coconut trunk, which, to put it
mildly, are not readily available in Paris *épiceries.*

The greatest of the Philippine fruits is the mango, but
even among Filipinos themselves it takes an adventurous
eater to track down the mysterious fruit called durian which
is cultivated by the Moslems of Mindanao, and for which
the eater must go to the fruit because the fruit won't come to
the eater. The smell beggars description, like very ripe
Liederkranz cheese but infinitely stronger, and it is so cling-
ing that airlines and many shipping lines refuse to transport
it. But if one has the courage to penetrate the fumes, the
meat is unexpectedly sweet, delicious, and addictive, and
once the taste is acquired, one can pine for durian when

one is far away. It is considered by the *datus* of Mindanao to be a virility fruit, which of course the Filipinos, with their huge population increases, need not at all.

One can go durian-hunting in Mindanao and watch Moslem fishermen sail their colorfully painted boats from Davao and Zamboanga, swimming from beaches as superb as any in Hawaii.

A dish that is more adventurous still is the *balut,* an egg that contains the almost hatched chick, served hot. Peddlers sell the egg from baskets in the central Luneta Park, and the unwary traveler may buy one thinking he is buying merely—an egg! Result: consternation, and often a rush for the toilet.

From Manila itself one can make many sorties and find rich rewards. One can take a forty-minute hydrofoil trip to Corregidor, scene of the classic battle of 1942 between the Americans and the Filipinos against the Japanese. It is preserved in the exact condition it was in when it was finally recaptured by the Americans. Its guns and the long, reinforced galleries, especially the famous Malinta Tunnel, make one wonder how any soldiers could have captured it at all.

Filipinos always insist that the visitor make at least one visit to the hill station of Baguio, with its golf courses, tennis courts, and playgrounds. It is not always easy for foreigners to comprehend the almost mystical importance of Baguio to Filipinos. Like Manila itself, Baguio seems to be a monument to the inability of the Philippines to avoid calamity. It was given a saturation bombing during the war, and it was there that General Yamashita surrendered, subsequently to

be executed for his atrocities to the Filipinos. Today new
buildings, and ramshackle, nondescript cottages stand side
by side with gutted ruins. But hidden behind the trees are
the elegant villas, impeccable lawns, and tennis courts of the
government ministers and wealthy Filipinos enjoying the
cool breezes from the five-thousand-foot elevation of the
town. From Baguio one can visit the fantastic primitive rice
terraces covering the mountains for as far as the eye can see,
one of the wonders of the world.

Taking into account the hot climate and the Malay tend-
ency to indolence, the Filipinos are unexpectedly athletic.
The favorite sport is basketball, which is odd for people who
are generally small in stature, but their tastes vary widely
to include a love for polo and golf among the wealthy residents of Forbes Park, Manila, for baseball and bicycle riding
among the ordinary people, and for headhunting among the
untamed tribes of the mountains of Luzon. A Filipino has
already held the world featherweight boxing title and no
one should be surprised—although everyone *will* be—when
the Philippines one day triumphs in some major international sporting competition. It may be the Davis Cup, or the
Masters' Golf Tournament, or even the Tour de France; the
author has persistently urged friends on the Manila newspapers to send a few of the country's crack cyclists to com-
pete, but France in the Filipino consciousness is as far away
as the moon.

Filipinos take their sport very seriously, and when the
Olympics or various Asian games fall due, national excitement reaches fever level. And then they have the habit of not
quite making it, of invariably, to quote the old reverse cliché,

snatching defeat from the jaws of victory, thus causing deep anguish in the press.

Such ricochets between keen anticipation and deep despair are common to most of the nations of the world. It is interesting to speculate why the United States is one of the few nations in the world which do not consider defeat in sport a national disaster; one reason possibly being that America is much less exposed to defeat, its major sports, baseball and football, being national rather than world-wide in appeal.

The sporting failures of the Philippines have a uniquely Asian quality. India, even more than the Philippines, had until a few years ago a similar tradition of dilettante athletic brilliance which never quite materialized in international competition. In both India and the Philippines it seems as if the national debilitation caused by dire poverty and exploding populations seeps upward into the bloodstream of even the well-nourished young men and women who can devote themselves seriously to sport. In international events they appear curiously fragile, and against the thunderous physical vigor of the Americans, Australians, and Russians they tend to crumple. But in the late sixties and the seventies, the Indian potential realized itself with magnificent international victories in tennis and cricket. The Philippine day will come.

In the meantime, affluent Filipinos rise early to play. Visitors who happen to be awake at such an hour are invariably astonished to see the golf courses and tennis courts busy at five o'clock in the morning as the players seek to beat the daytime heat.

But the real Philippine sporting passion, if one can call it sport at all, is, as it has been for centuries, cockfighting. Brought to the Philippines by the Chinese, it was adopted by the Spaniards, who introduced the gambling element which turned it into a national opiate. In every town and village, the cockpit, after the church, is the most familiar landmark. It is not a structure intended for aesthetes—usually a ramshackle affair of bamboo and wood, two or three stories high, and covered with a roof of tin or grass.

The cockfights are held on Saturdays, Sundays, and holidays, from mid-morning until sunset. Before the fight begins, the bookie goes into the pit, and in a chaotic and colorful ceremony, calls the odds. He is known as the *kristo* because of the Christlike posture he assumes, and the ear-splitting betting begins. Although the *kristo* commits nothing to paper he remembers the face of every bettor. Betting is on the honor system, and no afficionado ever welshes. The *kristo* is followed by the *sentenciador* or cockpit judge, and the fighting cocks hurl themselves at each other, six-inch razor-sharp blades attached to their left legs. The fight is to the death. If a fowl runs away the opponent wins. Sometimes both cocks die at the same time and the *sentenciador* declares the fight a draw. Traditionally the vanquished cock appears on the dinner table of the owner of the winner. A championship cock can cost two hundred dollars, and is cared for as lovingly as though it were a thoroughbred racehorse. A really great cock may survive up to four or five fights.

On a far gentler and more agreeable level, the Philippines has its own exquisite dance forms and its most famous dance company, the Bayanihan (meaning neighborhood) National Ballet of the Philippines has played all over the world. The most spectacular Filipino dance is the *tinikling,* a very evocative word for precisely timed steps by barefoot male and female dancers, between bamboo poles rapidly clapped together.

Despite the exotic setting, an American finds himself quickly at home in Manila. American standards seem to prevail everywhere—in the shops, drugstores, hotels, restaurants (although the sign in every restaurant cloakroom, "Please check your firearms before entering," does tend to make an American look twice).

The press, until it was put under government control by President Ferdinand Marcos's decree of martial law in 1972, was the freest and brashest in the world.

Television follows the American practice of sandwiching occasional programs between endless commercials.

Because the Philippine educational system is patterned after the American, social intercourse between Filipinos and Americans flows automatically. Indeed, it is the educational system that united the United States, the Philippines, and Canada. Few people know that. But then few people realize that the Filipinos speak English. With so much going for the Philippines, in education, culture, cuisine, sport, lifestyle, history, and tradition, it is one of the more heart-rending facts of life that everything always seems to go so wrong.

Chapter 2

THE SPANIARDS ARRIVE

A QUARTER OF a million years ago, in all probability, the first human beings showed their faces in what are now the Philippine Islands. Stone implements and other artifacts indicate the existence of people who resembled the Java Man. As these human-type figures implanted themselves in the islands they did not so much merge into society as impale themselves as separate entities, remaining the way they were, with remarkably little integration. As recently as 1972, a Stone Age tribe, the Tasadays, was discovered in the depths of the rain forests of Mindanao, 650 miles south of Manila, a little group of brown-skinned, lovable and loving little men, women, and children, free of hostility and intensely egregious, wearing only loincloths. They spoke a remote Malayo-Polynesian tongue and were found to be without metal technology or weapons to kill. They are now being carefully protected by the government.

The Stone Age people were followed about thirty thousand years ago by the Negritoes, and their descendants still survive, only marginally more advanced than the Tasadays, small men and women, often less than five feet tall, with dark, tightly curled hair, inhabiting remote mountain areas.

These were followed by the Mongoloid people from China. Rice-growing specialists, they arrived some five hundred years before the birth of Christ with a technology unequaled anywhere else on earth, and built their famous, unbelievably sophisticated rice terraces in the Mountain Province of Northern Luzon, which are classed among the eight man-made wonders of the world for the technical excellence of their irrigation, as efficient today as when they were first constructed.

But the largest and most dominant migration occurred from approximately 300 to 200 B.C., the Malays, traveling in great canoes up the coast of Borneo and by way of the Sulu Archipelago in the south, bringing their own considerable civilization: iron tools, pottery, and weaving skills.

Many other peoples followed, through both ancient and modern times, and into the twentieth century itself, these last being Chinese, Spanish, American, and even a small, though discernible, number of Japanese. They rarely mingled, so the country did not fuse into one, but instead developed into the richest cocktail of cultural minorities in the world, nearly all developing separately and with differing speed and success. There are today fifty-six ethnic groups, speaking seventy languages and dialects, of which the principal are Tagalog, Visayan, Cebuano, and Ilocano. The official language of business and politics is English, and the two languages of polite society are Spanish and English.

For most students of history, the history of the Philippines began in the spring of 1521 with the arrival of Ferdinand Magellan, in the course of the first circumnavigation of the world. He made his landfall at Cebu. Cebu was no deserted, undiscovered cove. Magellan found it bustling with commerce, the harbor crowded with the ships of China, Indonesia, and even India, exchanging cargoes, loading and unloading. At Mactan he discovered two tribal chieftains feuding, one of whom professed to adopt Christianity to win Magellan to his aid. The ruse succeeded. Magellan sought to mediate, and was killed by the other chieftain, by name Lapu Lapu. Magellan was forty-one years old. Only one of the ships of his squadron made its way back to Seville to complete the voyage around the world, but Magellan's task had been successfully accomplished. What he had done was cross that part of the world's water that was quite unknown. The rest of the way back to Europe, by way of the Indian Ocean and the Cape of Good Hope, was already known to, and charted by, the Portuguese. Historians consider the death of Magellan a tragedy, the trivial and unnecessary termination to a magnificent endeavor. The Filipinos see it quite differently. While they revere Magellan, they revere also the spirit of independence of Lapu Lapu who refused to be intimidated by these daunting adversaries. The death of Magellan is celebrated today in the Philippines as the first example of Asian resistance to European aggression, and Lapu Lapu is commemorated as the first national hero of the country.

Curious Portuguese adventurers began arriving in the islands in large numbers almost immediately afterward, but, as in Latin America, the first real break with the pagan past was made by those magnificent creators and destroyers of history, the Spanish conquistadors who landed in 1561, forty years after Magellan's death. In 1565, Miguel Lopez de Legazpi arrived with his "Soldiers of the Cross and the Sword," not with the bloody thunder of Pizarro in Peru, but more diplomatically, winning over chieftain after chieftain to the concept of Spanish sovereignty and the Church of Rome. Doubtless they had learned from Magellan's example that it was better to convert than to tangle.

Legazpi found the archipelago uncomfortably full of Portuguese bravos, and he established his headquarters at Manila, which was protected by a curious little island guarding and dominating the entrance to Manila Bay. This natural fortress he called Corregidor (the g pronounced ch as in the German "Aachen"), which is Spanish for "corrector" or "magistrate."

The conversion of the islands to Christianity was accomplished with the speed and efficiency to which the Spaniards had become accustomed, and by the turn of the century, the archipelago was firmly Christianized, save in Mindanao, Sulu, and Palawan where Mohammedanism was already established. The origin of Islam in the Philippines is not wholly clear. According to oral tradition it was brought to the people of Pulangi by one Kabungsuwan, a cadet of the ruling House of Johore in the fourteenth century. It also attracted princes who gave the Moslems a cohesion and a ferocity which the more peaceful people of the North had not attained.

The Spanish called these people "Moros," for "Mohammedan" or "Moor," against whom the Spaniards had been fighting for seven centuries. Although the Mohammedans were still unconquered, the Spanish claimed suzerainty over the entire territory which it called the Philippines, after Philip II.

For the most part, the pagan Filipinos, who lacked organized doctrine or an established priesthood, accepted Christianity eagerly. The Augustinians landed first, agog to convert, followed by the Franciscans in 1577, the Jesuits in 1581, the Dominicans in 1587, and the Augustinian Recollects in 1606. As each group arrived, the government administration assigned portions of the islands for them to evangelize. For the friars, conversion to the Church was its own reward, but for the soldiers disappointment was quick. They found no silver, no gold, only a certain amount of cinnamon, a poor reward for empire-building, in a place as remote from civilization as it was possible to be.

The enterprise, which might have foundered early from disinterest and the lack of reward was saved by two factors: the importance attached by the Church to the evangelizing of the heathen, and the magnificence of the port of Manila, with its deep water and rich hinterland. Behind the city, the areas of Laguna, Bulacan, and Pampanga were fertile enough to support a large urban population, and Pampanga provided the finest ship timber in the world. Legazpi and his successors ringed the city with great walls which still survive. The fortifications proved impregnable for more than a hundred years until they were made obsolete by the eighteenth century siege gun, but they continued to make a natural defense for the Japanese against the Americans and Filipinos in 1945.

Almost inevitably, Manila's value became that of an *entrepôt,* a great warehouse handling goods moving into and out of the Philippines—galleons piled with Chinese silks and porcelains, Burma jewels, East Indian spices, camphor wood from Formosa and Cambodian ivory, all bound for the Americas. But very little of this wealth seeped through to the ordinary people of the islands.

The hazards of such a distant offshoot of the Spanish Empire were huge. English privateers, commanded by men of the caliber of Sir Francis Drake, roamed the oceans for Spanish loot; Thomas Cavendish and his rapacious sailors captured one ship containing 250,000 pesos. The Moros of Mindanao were also seafarers, which, in the context of the time, meant pirates. For the Moros the islands were poor in everything except one single commodity: human beings. The princes raided the Visayan Islands and supplied the slave markets of southeast Asia with captives.

The Spanish resisted desperately, for very survival, and although they ultimately succeeded, their successes exhausted the islands as much as any conquerors would have done. The galleys of the king of Spain in this period were rowed by men torn from their families, chained to the oar and driven by the lash. Their wages were collected from their own villages as a war tax, and pocketed by the collectors. The king's rice, for the officials, was demanded in such quantities that the peasants who grew it had to subsist on palm shoots and bananas.

After the year 1600, the English menace receded somewhat, but immediately afterward the Dutch appeared on the horizon, marauders even more deadly and avaricious than the English. The Spanish conquistadors could, in one campaign, suppress the Moros, and then turn on the Dutch and repel them, too, but each campaign drained away more good men and money than the administration and the exchequer could stand, and wages were sometimes five years in arrears.

Ironically, the Spaniards were saved by China, a nation not considered the friendliest. The Chinese wanted Mexico's silver. In return the Chinese supplied the Spaniards with everything from gunpowder to wheat, and somehow the Spanish foothold was maintained, even though, for most of the seventeenth century, the inland waterways of the Philippines were abandoned to the Moros. Watchtowers still stand today, built by the missionaries to signal the approach of raiders; villagers would take to the hills, often leaving their property behind.

So much activity, whatever the strain imposed, had one inevitable result, namely that as middlemen the merchants of Manila, both Spanish and mestizo—those of mixed Spanish and Philippine blood—became rich. Because all the goods were imported, and then re-exported, and the rewards for such enterprises were galleons full of silver dollars, the humble local industries, fisheries and farming, were neglected, and as the merchants became richer, the rest of the country subsided into ever-deepening debt and serfdom.

The Chinese help brought huge problems of its own, notably the integration of the Chinese by the thousands, arriving in junks laden with riches, and then staying. When the Spaniards established Manila as a base of operations in 1571, they listed sixty Chinese families. By 1596 they were deporting up to 12,000 Chinese a year, but seven years later were obliged to plot an artificial massacre which thinned out the Chinese population by 23,000. Still the Chinese multiplied. On their side, they had the unarguable power of commerce. No Chinese, no galleon trade; no galleon trade, no money. It was as simple as that. A person living in those times and by enchantment reborn to see the islands today would find much about the Philippines that was very familiar. Today the rather indolent Malays worry about their hard-working Chinese compatriots as much as their ancestors did three hundred years ago, and the Philippine Army still makes forays into Mindanao to keep the Moros in check. And successive administrations continue to fret over the peonage of the peasants.

The Manila trade aside, there were few glittering fortunes to be made out of the Philippine Islands. As the excitements of war, booty, and Christianization wore away, the soldiers and priests who came to the Philippines found themselves there not on some great mission, but because Madrid had ordered them to go. The colony was an afterthought, a dumping ground of the Spanish Empire, attracting not the best or the most adventurous of the Spaniards, but the Spaniards who, in the modern idiom, had failed to make it. Manila for the Spaniard was the kiss of death, involving a two-year journey across two oceans and the continent of Central America, and, once the journey was completed, it was the end of the line, the point of no return.

Failed Spaniards came to the Philippines to die, but before dying felt they had the right to make life as comfortable as possible for themselves even if their comfort was to be at the expense of the natives. The trusting Filipinos were usually quite happy to oblige, and much too polite to protest.

The Spaniards introduced to the fascinated Filipinos two institutions of which they had never heard before—the *encomienda,* and the *repartimiento.* The *encomienda* was a royal grant to a Spanish colonist, not of property but of territory and its native inhabitants. The colonist defended his *encomienda* from attack, maintained peace and order, supported the missionary friars. In consideration for these valuable services to the Crown he acquired the right to collect tribute from the natives. The *repartimiento* entitled him to ask of the villages a fixed number of laborers for a fixed period.

The Filipinos did not know the scantiness of their luck. How could they? Maintaining even the barest communication even within the islands was difficult enough, and their only source of outside information and culture was either through the Church or through embittered Spanish colonialists. And even this information was received by way of Mexico, strained, as it were, through a filter. Direct communication with Spain did not exist.

Because the Spanish colonist, unlike his English rivals, intermarried freely with the natives, it took only a few generations for a considerable mestizo community to appear, part Malay, part Mediterranean, snobbish and sometimes ridiculous people, but with much potential power and intelligence, adopting Spanish dress and European customs, and speaking Spanish among themselves, leaving Tagalog and the other dialects to the domestics. They were allowed by the Spanish to choose their own Spanish names, often selecting them from the Madrid tax lists.

The conditions of life for the peasants were harsh, but tribute must be made to the Catholic friars, more so because, as the history of the Philippines progresses, their part becomes steadily less noble and more repressive. In the first two hundred years their energy and enthusiasm, their ingeniousness and their Christian dedication were impressive. They roamed the land building churches and organizing fiestas to honor the local saints. They plausibly incorporated earlier pagan rites and customs into their religious observances. If they did not actually proclaim that the act of baptism had miraculous powers to heal the sick, a great many Filipinos believed that it did, and flocked to the baptismal fonts.

In all the *barrios* the friars created spacious plazas with strong stone churches patterned on the Spanish baroque, a

similar pattern to be found in villages throughout the
country. They made the village fiesta the most important
occasion of the year, prepared and designed months in advance, the costumes stitched in the homes, the fireworks
ordered from Manila. It provided a whole week of religious
pomp, celebration, carousing, and drinking, at the end of
which the peasants were excessively hung over, and deeper
in debt than ever to the Church, the landowners, and the
Chinese moneylenders who thrived in every *barrio*.

To the Filipinos of all classes and education, the Church
was, and is, a beautiful thing; the Filipino God a flamboyant,
fun-loving God, existing deep in the individual soul, a God
who loves Filipinos and enjoys nothing better than a noisy
fiesta, and turns a tolerant blind eye to the cruelty of cockfighting.

The continuing ignorance of the Filipinos was one of the
principal sources of strength of the friars. Early in the nineteenth century, a remarkable document was circulated
anonymously, signed simply *"el indio agraviado"* (the
wronged Indian), who wrote:

> This is what you Spaniards are saying among yourselves; if we
> allow the Indians to learn Spanish, some may turn out to be
> satirists and scholars . . . if we allow them to prosper they will
> become rich, aspire to high and important posts and become per-
> sons of distinction. . . . Let us not teach them Spanish, let us
> leave them in ignorance. Let us not help them correct the bar-
> barous speech and stupid ideas that pass for polite conversation.
> Let them always be needy, that they may learn to steal. Thus
> we will be able to call them thieves because they will *be* thieves.
> And if—by a miracle—they refrain from stealing, being in need,

they will do what work they can for whatever wages they can
get. . . . By this method we will always be masters, and they
will always be poor, miserable, and ignorant . . .

The judgment is searing, but difficult to censure. The
friars, guarding their privileges, discouraged young Filipinos
from entering the priesthood, a wise precaution because it
was from the native, Philippine friars of the nineteenth century that the first major moves toward national independence were made, and from their ranks that the nation's first
martyrs were to be selected.

Chapter 3

THE *ILUSTRADOS*

THIRTEEN YEARS AFTER the American Revolution, the Stars and Stripes flew for the first time over Philippine waters. On October 3, 1796, an American ship registered in Salem, Massachusetts, sailed into Manila Bay, stayed for sixty-eight days, and then left for home, carrying a cargo of sugar, indigo, and pepper. The journey was made under hazardous conditions, as United States ships could not move freely on the high seas. The British Royal Navy, alarmed at the military successes of Napoleon Bonaparte, was stopping American merchant vessels, and forcibly impressing members of the crews into Royal Naval service.

To counter the British domination of the Atlantic, the merchants and shipbuilders of Salem combined money and craftsmanship to build fast merchantmen, which eluded the

British and sailed to the Orient by way of Cape Horn or the Cape of Good Hope.

The name of the ship is not on record, but the date was almost exactly one hundred years before the Philippines rose against the Spanish and opened the door to admit the United States to their country. The nineteenth century, the century of the world's awakening, was beginning for the Philippines, symbolically, as it ended, with the wave of the Yankee flag.

Almost as soon as the century began, the Spanish Empire, under heavy pressure from Napoleon, was obliged painfully and reluctantly to concede some new liberties to its overseas people. At the conference which drew up the Constitution of Cadiz in 1812, before Napoleon had turned his attention east toward Moscow, the Spanish government declared that, among other concessions, the peoples of the Empire would share full Spanish citizenship with the Spanish of the Peninsula. The Filipinos misunderstood this completely. The better-educated among them wondered if this provision meant that they would no longer have to pay tribute and forced labor to the Spanish, and the governor had some difficulty in explaining to them that this was not quite what Madrid had in mind.

In 1819, Mexico won independence from Spain, and the effect on the Philippines was prompt and decisive. It ended Manila's special place in Empire commerce as an *entrepôt,* and opened the port more fully to world trade. Almost immediately, native Philippine products, such as Manila hemp for rope, came into demand throughout the world. Sugar exports multiplied, creating more wealthy merchants in Panay, Negros, Luzon, and Batangas. For the first time, the more privileged Filipino families were able to widen their intellectual horizons and began to send their sons abroad for their education. The movement, once it started, could not be stopped or even slowed, and it was to gain tremendous momentum after November 1869, when the Suez Canal was opened, providing the Philippines with direct contact to Europe around the other side of the globe.

Until the nineteenth century, the prosperous mestizo families had been tolerated with a certain condescension by the Spanish colonists, and had been their willing accomplices in making sure that the peasants kept their place. Nevertheless, it was from this class that the movement toward independence gathered speed in the course of the century.

A new, and delightful, class was being born—that of the handsome young Filipinos of leisure—Malay Byrons—who studied the philosophies and realized that thoughts and political movements were afoot in Europe far beyond those imposed on the untutored Philippine archipelago by the suffocating rule of Madrid. Their worldly sophistication and their frequent dilettantism were balanced by burning patriotic passion and unquestioning religious faith. The friars might be resented and even hated; the Church never; and Madrid almost never. Spain was the mother of Philippine culture, and while her children might be gross, indifferent, and oppressive, the mother was always beautiful.

These young men became known as the *ilustrados,* and

they dreamed of Madrid as others dreamed of Paris, or Tchekov's three sisters dreamed of Moscow. Their influence was to dominate Philippine thinking, with intervals, to the present day, and to the rule of the incumbent *ilustrado* President, Ferdinand Marcos.

Independence came gradually to the Philippines in the nineteenth century, in a series of lurches, and with many setbacks. Each lurch threw up heroes and martyrs to enrich the Philippine history books. The first lurch became known as the Secularization Movement, from 1855 to 1872, characterized by the struggle of the Philippine clergy, under the leadership of Padre José Burgos, to Filipinize the parishes, and reduce Spanish injustices.

Father Burgos (1837–1872) was a good-looking Ilocano of a well-to-do family, and as a child prodigy won his Master of Arts degree at the age of seventeen. He then rose as high in the Church as it was possible for a Filipino to do, as curate to the Cathedral of Manila, and professor and master of ceremonies on the faculty of the University of Santo Tomas. Although he had effectively penetrated the Spanish ecclesiastical Establishment, and was now expected to conform with the Spanish priests, Father Burgos became increasingly rebellious because of the scornful attitude of the Spanish friars toward the native Filipino priests who were struggling honorably and under great difficulties to be worthy of their chosen vocation. The friars argued that the Tagalog was mentally inferior, and by reason of his race and idiosyncrasies, inefficient in the discharge of high duties. They asserted that the Filipino was an excellent soldier, a mediocre cor-

poral, a poor sergeant, and quite hopeless as officer material.
Similarly, so they said, the Filipino priest was incapable of
performing the more solemn priestly functions.

Burgos, in an article "To the Spanish nation," denied the
entire concept. He asserted, rightly, that there were many
secular priests who were far more capable than most friars,
many of whom were bored, cynical, and not particularly
literate themselves.

In January 1872, about two hundred Filipino soldiers re-
volted in Cavite, just south of Manila, killing their Spanish
commander. The revolt was quickly and brutally suppressed, and influential Spanish priests made the outbreak
an excuse to incriminate Burgos. He was charged with being
the spiritual leader and the mastermind of the uprising.
Burgos denied the allegations, but with two other priests,
Father Gomez, aged eighty-five, and Father Zamora, aged
thirty-seven, was sentenced to death. On the morning of
February 17, 1872, after a hasty trial, the three priests were
brought from Fort Santiago—a prison that has played as
notorious and recurring a part in Philippine history as the
Bastille in Paris—and in the presence of an enormous crowd
on Bagumbayan Field were garroted. Before the clamp was
fitted around his neck and the screw turned to cut the spinal
cord, Father Burgos, who was only thirty-five, gave confes-
sion to his executioner.

Father Burgos was perfect material for martyrdom—
young, dedicated, romantic. Yet he and all others are
dwarfed in historical stature by the next *ilustrado* to emerge
on the Philippine scene, and to lead what may be called the

second lurch for freedom, or what the Filipinos call the Propaganda Movement, from 1872 to 1892. His name was José Rizal.

The memoirs of a traveler, published shortly before the birth of Rizal, give a good indication of the life in which Rizal was raised. In 1859, an English visitor, Sir John Bowring, described in his book, *A Visit to the Philippine Islands,* his meeting with a prominent *ilustrado,* Don José Alberto of Biñang who, Bowring learned to his delight, had gone to school in, of all places, Calcutta, and spoke English fluently. Don José invited the Englishman to dinner. Bowring observed:

> His house was a very large one, and gave abundant evidence that he had not studied in vain the arts of domestic civilization. The furniture, the beds, the tables, the crockery were all in good taste. . . . Great crowds were gathered in the square which fronts Don José Alberto's house. Indians brought their game cocks to be admired. . . . There was much firing of guns . . . and a large fire balloon, bearing the inscription, "The people of Biñang to their illustrious visitors" soaring aloft, was lost sight of in the distance . . .

Don José Alberto, it so happened, had a sister who had married into a family in the friendly and neighboring province of Calamba, and produced eleven children. The seventh of these children, born two years after the visit of Sir John Bowring, was José Rizal.

Don José Rizal Mercado y Alonzo (the two last names are those of his mother and grandfather, a Spanish form) grew up to be the supreme *ilustrado,* a Renaissance man who could do anything to which he turned his hand and mind.

In the course of a short life, terminated by a firing squad at
the age of thirty-five, he became the greatest eye surgeon in
Asia, a distinguished sculptor, an agrarian, a poet, a linguist,
a propagandist, and author of one of the classic novels of
world literature, *Noli Me Tangere*—meaning "Touch Me
Not." Rizal learned the alphabet at three, and at five could
read and understand the Bible. At eight he was composing
poems in Tagalog. In 1882, when he was twenty-one, he left
the Philippines for Spain and was introduced to the whole
wondrous culture of Europe. In Madrid and Germany he
graduated first as a Doctor of Philosophy and Letters, and
then as a doctor and an eye specialist. In London he haunted
the Reading Room of the British Museum—just as the exiled
Lenin did twenty years afterward—studying the pre-Spanish
culture of the Philippines, seeking evidence of the sources
of the potential greatness he saw in his own country. The
principal object of his research was to disprove the friars'
teachings that the Filipinos, before the Spaniards arrived,
were savages living in trees. He fell in love with, and almost
married, an English girl. He learned to speak no fewer than
twenty-two languages: all the major European languages,
plus Latin, Arabic, Malayan, Sanskrit, Hebrew, Catalan,
Chinese, Japanese, Tagalog, Ilocano, Visayan, and Subano
(the language of the people of Cebu).

In Berlin he completed his great novel, *Noli Me Tangere.*
The words are those of Jesus to Magdalen at the sepulcher,
and are generally given as a warning against interference.
Noli Me Tangere is a superb novel, a witty and devastating

satire on the Spanish in the Philippines, and a savage attack on the abuse of church power. The ordinary reader, and even certain scholars, can be excused for passing this great work by. Written in Spanish, it suffered for more than half a century from abysmal translations which unfortunately still circulate. English-language students are advised to avoid all save that of León Ma. Guerrero. Dr. Guerrero is a Philippine diplomat who undertook the translation while serving in the Philippine Embassy in London in the 1950s, an undertaking which in itself illustrates the continuing *ilustrado* tradition among educated Filipinos.

Rizal followed *Noli Me Tangere* with a sequel, *El Filibusterismo,* which also benefits from a Guerrero translation, and is worthwhile reading without carrrying the wit or the tremendous power of the first book. Guerrero, not very satisfactorily, translates the title as *The Hustler*.

Rizal arrived back in the Philippines in advance of his books, which the Spanish Establishment had not yet had the occasion to read. He was welcomed home as an international celebrity, received by the governor and borne from province to province in triumph by his friends. He opened a clinic in Calamba, performed a successful and delicate operation on his mother's eyes, and rich patients came from all over the archipelago to consult him.

The Manila he had returned to, as described in *Noli Me Tangere* was a colorful, vibrant and an alarming city:

> The hustle and bustle everywhere, so many carriages and cabs at a dash, Europeans, Chinese, and natives, each dressed after

their own fashion, fruit peddlers, messengers, porters stripped to the waist, foodshops, inns, restaurants, shops, carts pulled by philosophical carabaos, the noise, the incessant movement, the sun itself, a certain smell, the riot of colors—he had almost forgotten what Manila was like.

The streets had still not been paved. Let the sun shine two days in a row, and they dissolved into clouds of dust that covered everything, blinding passersby and sending them into fits of coughing; let it rain a day, and the streets become a marsh, gleaming at night with the reflected lanterns of carriages that splashed mud on the pedestrians on the narrow sidewalks as far as five meters away. How many women had lost their embroidered slippers in that sea of mud! In time the chain-gangs would show up to repair the streets; shaven-pated men wearing short-sleeved shirts and knee-length pants, letters and numbers in blue, chained in twos, grimy rags wrapped round their ankles against the friction of the fetters or perhaps the coldness of the steel, burnt by the sun, driven to exhaustion by the heat, their exertions, and the whips of the trusties who derived their particular pleasure from flogging their fellows. The prisoners were usually tall men with stern faces whose eyes flashed when the whip fell whistling across their shoulders, or when a passerby tossed them a cigar butt, damp and shredded, to be picked up by the nearest and hidden in his straw helmet, while his fellows watched the other passersby with unfathomable looks. . . .

The pontoon bridge was gone. It had been a good bridge for all its faults, rising and falling with the tides of the River Pasig which more than once had battered and destroyed it . . . The almond trees in the square of San Gabriel were as thin as ever. The Escolta, the main business street, seemed less attractive than when he had last seen it, in spite of a new building decorated with draped female figures, which had taken the place of a group of warehouses . . . He met many carriages drawn by teams of magnificent ponies, carrying businessmen on their way to work, still half asleep, military men, Chinese in foolish and ridiculous postures, grave friars, canons, in elegant, open carriages. . . .*

Then, as the old joke goes, the other shoe dropped for Rizal. *Noli Me Tangere* arrived in the islands, and the outraged friars declared that it advocated the violent overthrow of the government. A committee of the faculty of the University of Santo Tomas, and the Permanent Censorship Committee found it "libelous, immoral and pernicious," banned it from the bookshops, and urged that the author should be severely punished. Rizal left the Philippines again, somewhat hurriedly, and returned to Europe.

In London he wrote articles urging the Spanish government to grant reforms to the Philippines. He did not advocate independence as such, and he expressly opposed violence of any kind. He moved to Madrid and joined the colony of Philippine exiles, writing articles, in one of which he forecast that, within a century, the Philippines would fall either to the North American Republic or to the Japanese, a prophecy that was to be fulfilled in both respects in less than half a century.

Through these years, Rizal remained a bachelor, which was unusual for a Filipino. To this day, they all delight in early marriage and huge families. He was an ardent lover and broke hearts on both sides of the globe without ever—quite—becoming a philanderer. His parents were aging and he resolved to return to the Philippines despite warnings of

* Originally published in London by Longmans Green and Co., Ltd., and reprinted by permission of the translator, the Honorable León Ma. Guerrero.

danger from his friends. Not only did he return but, in the
circumstances, behaved with considerable rashness. He organized La Liga Filipina to "unite the Filipino people for
the promotion of industry, education, and agriculture." The
administration quickly seized on this action to have him
thrown into Fort Santiago, and then banished to the distant
town of Dapitan in Zamboanga, where he went accom-
panied by a pretty Irish mistress, and trailed, liked the Pied
Piper of Hamelin, by people from all over Asia seeking treat-
ment for their eye infections.

Rizal, not without reason, seemed to have a fatalistic pre-
monition of his own impending martyrdom, and came to a
decision that many, in the hindsight of history, found remarkable, but those understanding his romantic, impulsive
nature could recognize as totally logical. When the Spanish-
American War broke out in May 1898, he volunteered to
serve as a surgeon in the Spanish Army in Cuba, and was
accepted. The fact is that he was probably bored to distrac-
tion in Dapitan. He wanted to see action, and doubtless
wanted to study the Spanish influence in Cuba as compared
with that in the Philippines, the two countries being almost
all that was left of the once huge Spanish Empire. He set
sail for Barcelona in a Spanish warship. In Singapore friends
pleaded with him to quit the ship and seek asylum under
the protection of the British Empire which he admired so
much. Rizal declined. He was arrested in mid-ocean and sent
back to the Philippines in the first mail-boat from Barcelona.

The court martial in Manila was a farce. He was charged
with joining subversive organizations, and automatically

found guilty. In fact, he was guilty only of the sin of writing a book which the friars did not like. Book critics are rarely so powerful. As Dr. Guerrero points out in the introduction to *Noli Me Tangere,* had the trial taken place fifty years later, under a more jovial colonial administration, Rizal would have served a term in jail and emerged to become Prime Minister of his country. But the Spaniards are not a people given to accommodation. Rizal was sentenced to death and confined to Fort Santiago, where he wrote the beautiful and patriotic poem, "Mi Ultimo Adios" (My Last Farewell). On December 30, 1896, he was taken out and, before a large crowd, was cut down by a firing squad of Filipino colonial troops. As in the case of Father Burgos a quarter of a century earlier, the Spaniards had accorded martyrdom not to violent men brandishing bolos, but to men devoted to peace who were rash enough to cross their own masterly intellects with the poor intellects of their colonial rulers. The execution of Rizal was almost the last gasp of the Spaniards in Asia. Even if Commodore Dewey's American naval squadron had not appeared on the horizon eighteen months later to deliver the *coup de grâce,* it is doubtful if Spain could have maintained its crumbling hold on a nation now, at last, after three and a half centuries, ripe for independence.

Chapter 4

THE STRUGGLE FOR FREEDOM

THE EXECUTION OF Rizal marked the beginning of violent revolution. He had ignited the Filipino people and made them believe in themselves. For the first time, truly, they saw themselves as he saw them, a real people, of "sensitivity and pride," his own words.

The revolution quickly fell into the classic pattern of revolution everywhere, before and since: two-pronged, with double purposes, double aims, and considerable double-crossing; philosophy entangled in militancy, martyrdom degraded by massacre, idealism by assassination. Even so, it produced no real villains: no Robespierres, no Trotskys or Stalins. Such is the sunny Filipino temperament that even those who behaved most dubiously are still heroes in Filipino eyes. While Rizal conceived of his Liga Filipina as a peaceful forum for the achievement of reform, a powerful militant organization was forming alongside, The Supreme Worshipful Sons of the People, more popularly known under its Tagalog abbreviation as the Katipunan. Whereas the Liga was philosophical and donnish, the Katipunan was working-class and activist, born, not out of the Reading Room of the British Museum, but out of the slums of Manila and the poverty-obsessed *barrios*.

The leader of the Katipunan was a tough, self-educated young man, Andres Bonifacio (1863–1896), whose dreadful childhood would have reduced a lesser man to desperation and petty crime, and whose horrible death is posthumously compensated by his position in history as "the Great Plebeian," the father of the nation's drive to independence.

Bonifacio's portraits and photographs show him as stern and unsmiling, with a Napoleonic forelock, although his eyes seem to lack the fanaticism which burn in the eyes of, say, Lenin, or Fidel Castro. Bonifacio was born in the teeming Tondo section of Manila, on November 30, 1863. His parents could not afford to send him to school at all, but somehow he succeeded in struggling through second-year high school. At that stage in his life, both parents died, and he had to support his brothers and sisters by making paper fans and walking-sticks which he peddled in the streets of Manila, accepting the kicks and the oaths along with the occasional centavos. He was married at twenty, and became a widower almost immediately when his wife died of leprosy. He remarried, and the child of that marriage died of exposure.

For Bonifacio the only escape from the bleakness and dire

poverty of his youth lay in reading. He was particularly fascinated by the French Revolution, and he was also intrigued by the mysterious rites of freemasonry. His idol was José Rizal, who was two years his senior. He joined Rizal's Liga Filipina and, shocked by Rizal's exile to Dapitan, came to the conclusion that the only solution lay in the violent overthrow of Spanish rule. With a few colleagues of similar determination, he founded the Katipunan, its aims being largely that of the French revolutionaries, and its organization based on Masonic practices with secret names, signs, code words, and oaths of allegiance, signed in blood.

The Katipunan expanded with enormous rapidity, almost like a brush fire, indicating clearly that the centuries-long Philippine patience and fatalism were at breaking point. Estimates vary from 100,000 to 400,000 active members. On August 26, 1896, while Rizal was on the Spanish warship bound for Cuba, insurrection broke out at a noisy meeting of Katipuneros at the town of Balintawak. Bonifacio and his fierce followers tore up their Spanish identification documents, crying "Long live Philippine independence!" Although this, today, sounds as conventional as a football-game war-whoop, at that time it was as thrilling to the Philippine people as the storming of the Bastille to the French a century earlier. It has become known in Philippine history as "the Cry of Balintawak," commemorated with bravura on endless statues and postage stamps.

Intoxicated at the vision of impending independence, Bonifacio and a battalion of his Katipuneros, armed with bolo knives, stormed the Spanish garrison at San Juan del Monte

on August 30, in what was the first battle for Philippine independence. The engagement was bloody and all but ended
in victory for the Katipuneros. The Spanish garrison was
saved by last-minute reinforcements, forcing Bonifacio to
retreat. He attacked again at San Francisco de Malabon and
was again repulsed with heavy losses. It was at this point
that the Spanish administration in Madrid, close to panic,
decided that, had it not been for José Rizal's insidious writ-
ings, none of this would have happened. They ordered him
arrested while his ship was on the way to Barcelona, brought
him back and shot him, as a result of which the Katipunan
brush fire ignited into flames. From all the islands, both
men and women flocked to the ranks.

It is not often that a leader is challenged from within his
own ranks while he is at the height of his power and prestige, but that is what now happened to Bonifacio. One of
Bonifacio's most dashing field commanders was Emilio
Aguinaldo who, even then, believed that Bonifacio's mantle
of leadership would fit him very well.

Emilio Aguinaldo y Famy is one of the strangest, most
colorful, most enduring, and most tormented figures in
Philippine history. His light erupted like a magnesium flare
on the Philippine scene and was almost immediately extinguished, but the flash remains in Filipino eyes forever. He
was born in Cavite on the southern side of Manila Bay on
March 22, 1869, making him six years younger than Bonifacio. He was only twenty-seven when he distinguished himself in the battles of the Katipunan. Aguinaldo came from
a middle-class family, but was compelled to leave college in

his second year when his father died, and he returned home to engage in farming and business affairs. His adventurous spirit longed for action and he was one of the earliest members of the Katipunan. Even as a young man he was a strange-looking individual—small, with cold Oriental eyes, and a brush haircut flattened into a horizontal line at the top of his head, like Dick Tracy's classic character, Flattop.

His courage and determination were such that after the battles he acquired an influential following of his own, suggested, of all things, that the Katipunan was insufficiently militant, and proposed to replace it with a revolutionary government; a "government" being a giant step from a mere political-military movement. On March 22, 1897, a convention followed his wishes and appointed him President. The portfolio for military matters was given to a tough soldier named Artemio Ricarte, of whom more will be heard later, and Bonifacio, although he presided over the convention, found himself appointed to the post of Minister of the Interior, under Aguinaldo.

Bonifacio's rage was increased when a delegate, one Daniel Tirona, derided even that appointment, declaring that Bonifacio was not a lawyer and lacked education. Bonifacio hurled himself on Tirona and might have killed him if Artemio Ricarte had not separated them.

Bonifacio stormed out declaring that he would not recognize the conclusions of the convention. This was a dangerous split in the revolutionary movement. Bonifacio was still the idol of the Philippine masses, and if Aguinaldo was to consolidate his victory he had to act quickly. Bonifacio, with his elder brother, Ciriaco, and younger brother, Procopio, was on his way back to Manila, when they were overtaken on the road by a platoon of Aguinaldo's soldiers. They resisted arrest and guns were drawn. Two of the soldiers fell dead, and Ciriaco Bonifacio was also killed. Bonifacio was wounded and taken prisoner with his younger brother after bitter fighting. On May 4, they were tried and found guilty of treason and sedition. Aguinaldo had grave doubts as to the wisdom of shooting the nation's hero, and decided that the brothers should be exiled to some remote island. But hotheads among his generals persuaded him that the country could not afford to show a divided front, and Aguinaldo reluctantly agreed to the brothers' execution.

The two young men were being held in a house at Mount Buntis at the border of Cavite and Batangas, strong Aguinaldo territory. The execution platoon was led by one Major Makapagal, a professional officer trained under the Spaniards. When the brothers were led from their jail and Andres Bonifacio saw the execution squad lined up for the firing, he went on his knees to Makapagal, and begged for the lives of his brother and himself. Makapagal answered that, as a soldier, he had no alternative but to obey orders, and Procopio was dragged to the firing post and shot before his brother's eyes. Andres again went on his knees and pleaded that, as they had already shot his brother, his life should be spared for the sake of the Philippines. Then Bonifacio, seeing that the officer was not to be swayed from what he considered his duty, made a run for it. He made a certain amount of ground, but was slowed by his wounds, and in great pain. The soldiers trapped him in a dry creek and shot him down like a dog.

Bonifacio's death left Aguinaldo in undisputed command. He continued to campaign against the demoralized Spanish garrisons for much of 1897, and the Spanish, although given a psychological boost by the departure of Bonifacio, could never pin the astute Aguinaldo down. By the end of the year he had exhausted the Spanish and reduced the war to a stalemate. The Spanish had captured most of the territory once held by the rebels, including almost all of Aguinaldo's native province of Cavite, but Aguinaldo's men continued to control the mountains and the hours of darkness. An agreement was made. On December 14, 1897, just one year after the death of Rizal and seven months after the execution of Bonifacio, the Spanish signed a treaty with Aguinaldo which, the Spanish hoped, would settle the turmoil that had prostrated the archipelago for the past eighteen months. The terms of the treaty held that the Spanish would grant an amnesty and introduce social reforms among the Filipinos. They would pay an indemnity of 1,700,000 pesos, of which 900,000 were to be awarded to civilians whose property had been damaged, and the balance given to Aguinaldo and his senior officers, provided they quit the Philippines and, as it were, get lost. There is considerable mystery concerning what happened to the money. Some sources say that Aguinaldo received only 400,000 pesos. Aguinaldo later stated that every peso he received was used by him for the purchase of arms from Japan, though few if any Japanese arms were subsequently seen in action in the Philippines.

The war was temporarily over, but the Spanish breathing space did not last long. On May 1, 1898, a new power entered the Philippine scene, that of the United States of America, already at war with Spain. Three months earlier, in February, war had been precipitated by the sinking of the *U.S.S. Maine* in Havana Harbor under circumstances never satisfactorily explained. Younger men in the American administration of President McKinley realized that the Spanish Empire was crumbling away, and felt it imperative and urgent that the United States should fill the vacuum before the European powers did so. These Americans of vision were not worried about the existing colonial powers—the British, French, and Dutch who were glutted with global real estate —but they were very worried indeed about Germany and Japan, both of whom felt aggrieved that they had been left out of the race for colonies, and were impatient to make up for it. Commodore Dewey's squadron, at anchor in Hong Kong, was ordered to Manila to prevent the Spanish fleet from escaping to the high seas. Dewey slipped through the fortifications of Corregidor, sank the Spanish fleet without loss to himself, and found himself, at least temporarily, the master of the Philippines.

On hearing the news, President William McKinley dropped to his knees, and according to his own testimony, "prayed to Almighty God for light and guidance." McKinley needed such help, if only to understand the complicated and interlocking events which were to follow, and which will, here, be explained as simply as possible.

Aguinaldo, exiled from the Philippines, had made his

temporary home in Hong Kong, but he was on his way to Europe by boat when he heard the news from Manila. What happened next has yielded conflicting accounts. According to Aguinaldo he held a meeting in Singapore with the American Consuls of Singapore and Hong Kong who told him that if he returned to the Philippines and led his men against the Spanish as allies of the Americans, the United States would recognize the independence of the Philippines. Commodore, later Admiral, George Dewey denied that any such promise had been made.

Within three weeks, Aguinaldo was back in Cavite, his men supplied with arms and ammunition by Admiral Dewey, and in June he defeated the Spanish forces outside of Manila after a pitched battle. Meanwhile, the American forces landing in the Philippines, and raising the Stars and Stripes instead of the Spanish flag, were wildly cheered by the people, who hailed them as liberators.

In the same months, the independence of the Philippines was proclaimed for the first time, at Kawit, in the province of Cavite. General Aguinaldo unfurled the Philippine flag and played the Philippine national anthem. A temporary capital was established at Malolos, north of Manila, where, on September 15, 1898 a revolutionary Congress assembled to draw up the constitution of the Philippines. In the euphoria it had passed almost unnoticed that, on the other side of the world, American and Spanish diplomats were negotiating the Treaty of Paris which ceded the Philippines to the United States of America. Nevertheless, on January 23, 1899, Aguinaldo was unanimously elected the first President of the Philippine Republic by the eighty members of the Revolutionary Congress, who included some of the most distinguished civilians and scholars of the Philippines, a far cry from the wild warriors who had tumbled Bonifacio from power two years earlier. Emilio Aguinaldo was not quite thirty years old.

It might be thought that the *ilustrado* influence had waned since the death of Rizal; men like Bonifacio and Aguinaldo were men of violence rather than reflection. But this is not strictly true. The Filipino leaders still had deep respect for the nation's intellectuals like Mabini and Pardo y Tavera. Dr. Trinidad Pardo y Tavera was an especially interesting figure, commanding the respect of regime after regime, a kind of Filipino Talleyrand. Distinguished-looking, with a neatly trimmed beard, Tavera was the very model of the *ilustrado,* descendant of a Spanish noble family dating back to the fifteenth century. Educated in Paris, a doctor, like Rizal, and an intimate friend of Rizal, he was always among the intellectual leadership in the Philippine independence movement. He had counseled against the execution of Bonifacio, and although he was almost venerable by the youthful standards of Philippine leadership—he was in his forties—he served as a guerrilla fighter under Aguinaldo. He participated in the deliberations that led to the constitution and to the election of President Aguinaldo, but realized instantly that conflict with the United States would be disastrous for the Philippines. He saw that the only future for his country would be in cooperation with America, and he strove desperately to avert the new war that was approaching with terrifying speed and almost unstoppable force. His efforts were in vain.

A strong body of opinion in the United States opposed the annexation of the Philippines. The Democratic Party, then in opposition, denouncing American imperialism, made the Philippine affair an issue in domestic politics through several subsequent presidential campaigns. Those defending annexation argued that if the Americans stayed aloof the Filipinos would find themselves with rulers much stronger than the Spanish, and even less benign, namely the Japanese or the Germans or both.

On February 4, 1899, two weeks after his inauguration, Aguinaldo declared war on the United States in the name of the Philippine Republic, and so began a long-drawn-out, often bloody conflict, which became known to American schoolboys as "the Philippine Insurrection," and to many Filipinos as "the Philippine-American War."

In declaring war, Aguinaldo broke with Tavera who, with many other responsible Filipinos, accepted the American position. Tavera founded a pro-American newspaper, *La Democracia,* supporting the proposition that the American mission to the Philippines was to promote the well-being, prosperity, and happiness of the Filipino people.

From the outset, the superiority in weapons and training of the Americans enabled them to occupy the country much at will. As early as March 31, six weeks after the declaration of war, they captured Malolos, capital of the new republic. This was remarkably fast work when it is remembered that it took the Germans that long to reach Paris in 1940, in a campaign that gave birth to the expression "blitzkrieg." The American commander was General Arthur MacArthur, father of Douglas MacArthur.

But Aguinaldo's generals, veterans now of almost three years of scarcely interrupted combat, fought back with great skill, and inflicted heavy casualties. The three most distinguished were Artemio Ricarte, General Gregorio del Pilar, and General Antonion Luna. However, although they stood like Horatius at the bridge, where once there were three, in the end there were none. First to fall was Antonion Luna. Since he was unquestionably the best strategist on the Philippine side, Aguinaldo had made him commander in chief. After that, Luna's days were numbered. Luna, traveling to Cabanatuan for a conference with Aguinaldo, found nobody in the house they had agreed on for their rendezvous. Luna explored the various rooms, and making his way downstairs, was shot dead by Aguinaldo's gunmen. Rumors had been circulating for some time that Luna was plotting to oust his chief. The rumors then ceased, and Aguinaldo's leadership was no longer in dispute.

In November 1899, Aguinaldo, amid the decimation of his organization, ordered all his commanders to split up and resort to guerrilla warfare, and the bitterest part of the war began. Like the Viet Cong sixty years later, the Filipinos became experts at ambush—suddenly attacking and then fading into the countryside. Their principal weapons were Spanish rifles and bolo knives. Captured U.S. Army Krag-Jörgensen rifles were highly prized. They also created an odd-looking bamboo cannon loaded with scrap iron.

Wherever the U.S. Army struck, Aguinaldo was some-where else. Subsequent campaigns of the twentieth century produced many brilliant guerrilla leaders, such as Von Mac-kensen in German East Africa in World War I, Abd el Krim in the Rif mountain campaign against the French in Mo-rocco in the 1920s, Tito and his Yugoslav Partisans in World War II, and so on to the legendary General Giap of North Viet Nam. Emilio Aguinaldo is worthy company for the best of them.

Even so, his place in military history might have ended in December 1899, and coincided with the end of the nine-teenth century, had he not narrowly escaped capture. How-ever, fifty soldiers under General del Pilar covered his re-treat, and fought a brilliant rearguard action at Tirar Pass, Pilar dying with his men. That meant that two of Agui-naldo's best generals were dead.

The American troops, although better led than most regular armies of the time, were consistently outmaneuvered by the invisible enemy. To representatives of an army that had not been defeated since the birth of the American re-public, the frustration was particularly galling, and they developed a deep hatred for the "Flips" and the "Googoos" as they called them. They marched to a song set to the tune of "Tramp! Tramp! Tramp!," with the following words:

> *Damn! Damn! Damn the Filipinos.*
> *Cut-throat, khakiac ladrones!*
> *Underneath the starry flag,*
> *Civilize 'em with a Krag,*
> *And return us to our beloved homes.*

It is interesting to note, in passing, that on the eve of the twentieth century, the U.S. Army used the Spanish word, *ladron,* meaning a petty thief, or a robber, which was first used against the natives of the territory by Ferdinand Magellan.

As Dr. Trinidad Tavera had foreseen, however, the ultimate success of American arms was inevitable. The Filipinos continued to fight through the year 1900 and into the spring of 1901, and were bled white of men, arms, and money. They had lost 20,000 dead and had themselves killed 4,165 American troops. Aguinaldo was moving as skillfully as ever, but his hide-and-seek war with the Americans was being conducted in ever decreasing circles, and by 1901 had been pushed back into Palanan, in remote northern Luzon. From there he sent a confidential dispatch to his guerrilla commander in central Luzon, asking for reinforcements. The letter was intercepted, and the delighted Americans realized that Aguinaldo was now in their clutches if he did not slip out again, as he had done so often.

The operation that led to his capture was described by Theodore Roosevelt as requiring "iron courage." British military observers on the spot, however, described it as "not cricket."

The officer in charge of the operation was a well-known American swashbuckler of the period, Frederick Funston, a former newspaperman, then a general of the Kansas Volunteers, and a son of a Kansas congressman locally known as "Foghorn" Funston. In order to reach Palanan, Funston and his small force of mixed Americans and Filipinos loyal to the United States had to effect a nightmarish forced march through steaming, fever-filled jungles, and over mountains.

Once in Palanan they represented themselves to the natives as American prisoners being delivered by the Filipinos to General Aguinaldo. Deceived by a forged letter, Aguinaldo even sent the exhausted group supplies of food.

Some days later, on March 27, in the midst of a humid jungle morning, General Aguinaldo was sitting behind his desk in his headquarters in a nipa shack. Suddenly firing broke out in the compound, and Aguinaldo, furious, rushed to the window to shout to his men to stop wasting ammunition. When he turned back, he found himself looking down the barrel of a pistol. "You are my prisoner, General Aguinaldo," Frederick Funston told him. Aguinaldo in later years described Funston as a man "of great heart and fierce courage."

Aguinaldo was brought by his triumphant captors to Manila. There he agonized for a while in prison, wondering in which direction his duty and his destiny lay, and with a suddenness which surprised even the most knowledgeable students of his personality, he took the oath of allegiance to the American flag, just one week after his capture. This was on April 1, 1901, celebrated by many people as April Fool's Day. His decision was greeted with relief by many Filipinos, including Dr. Tavera, but with grief and shock by many more. The war did not end with Aguinaldo's capture. Filipino forces continued to fight the Americans in the mountains for more than a year, at the end of which

Aguinaldo's most distinguished lieutenant, Artemio Ricarte, declared he would never surrender to either Spaniard or American, and departed for Tokyo.

Aguinaldo was still only thirty-two years old. Whatever his ambitions were for the future, it can be said with confidence that they were never destined to be fulfilled. His life, so full of gore, glory, and adventure, and so short into the bargain, had effectively ended, even though he did not realize the fact at the time. It was tragic in that it fell so far short of tragedy. In Greek tragedy, the theme is of *hubris* followed by *nemesis,* but for Aguinaldo there was to be no nemesis, only a fading away that lasted longer than that of most old soldiers. He went into retirement, and made only occasional forays thereafter into public life, not always wise forays.

As he grew older he became more and more a living legend, consulted out of courtesy and out of respect for the nation's history. He received ambassadors and visiting dignitaries; he was visited as if he were some kind of national monument. He invariably received his visitors wearing a neat starched uniform. His manners were old-fashioned and courteous, and he spoke in a lilting, flowing Spanish. His hair grew gray, but remained thick, and he retained his table-mountain hairstyle with its horizontal top. The old warrior who had negotiated with President McKinley went on to outlive President John F. Kennedy. Although he had renounced the Catholic Church when he was fighting the Spanish, he became reconciled to it in the last months of his life, and he died in February 1964, after a long illness, at

the age of ninety-five. The father of his country, he was
buried with every honor, and with world-wide tributes, from
President Lyndon B. Johnson, General Douglas MacArthur,
former President Dwight D. Eisenhower, and innumerable
others.

Emilio Aguinaldo grew up in the Spanish colonial school
of ruthlessness, authoritarianism, and corruption. In his vital
years, it was the only school he knew, so he is not to be
judged by contemporary standards of fair play. He occupies
one of the most important places in Philippine history, and
of him it can be said that he was always too eager to accommodate, to live to fight another day, ever to have made the
Spaniards proud of him.

In all forms of government . . . the Commission should bear
in mind that the government which they are establishing is designed not for our [American] satisfaction or for the expression
of our theoretical views, but for the happiness, peace and prosperity of the people of the Philippine Islands, and the measures
adopted should be made to conform to their customs, their habits
and even their prejudices, to the fullest extent consistent with the
accomplishment of the indispensable requisites of just and effective government. At the same time the Commission should
bear in mind, and the people of the islands should be made
plainly to understand, that there are certain great principles of
government which have been made the basis for our govern-
mental system, which we deem essential to the rule of law and
the maintenance of individual freedom, and of which they have,
unfortunately, been denied the experience possessed by us; that
there are certain practical rules of government which we have
found essential to the preservation of these great principles of
liberty and law, and that these principles and these rules of
government must be established and maintained in their islands
for the sake of their liberty and happiness, however much they
may conflict with the customs or laws of procedure with which
they are familiar.

It is significant to compare these high sentiments with the
anguished cry of *el indio aggraviado* (the wronged Indian)
quoted earlier and written only a century before.

For Filipinos, their nerves and psyches still raw from four
years of war and three and a half centuries of Spanish rule,
the American occupation was a revelation for its benevo-
lence, good humor, and democratic motivation. Outside of
Mindanao, there was no blood-letting whatever. Although
Americans were in the majority of the first Philippine Supreme Court, the Chief Justice was a Filipino. William
Howard Taft, avoiding the temptation of all politicians to

consult yes-men and time-servers, turned for his advice to
the most sophisticated living Filipino, Dr. Trinidad Tavera,
who became his principal adviser and aide. Tavera's ambition for his country was one shared, in a less articulate way,
by many Filipinos. He wanted to see the Philippines so
Americanized that it would be admitted as one of the states
of the American Union.

Teaching, largely ignored by the Spanish, was given such
importance by the Americans that many astonished Filipinos
at first wondered what all the fuss was about; farming the
land required no books. The task was left, at first, to the
U.S. Army, and American soldiers proved to be willing educators, popular with Filipino children who later grew up to
be important and influential citizens. All of which was splendid for Philippine-American relations, but left a calami-
tously low standard of scholarship among many Filipinos.
Happily, the Army teachers were followed by the "Thomas-
ites," dedicated civilian teachers from the States, so-called
because they arrived on the U.S. Army transport *Thomas,*
and adopted the name as a badge of honor.

The teachers introduced the American system of education to the Philippines, very different from the *lycée* system
practiced in Europe. They also taught in English because,
for the majority, it was the only language they knew, apart
from high-school French, and Filipinos have rarely shown
the slightest interest in learning French. There was no de-
liberate planning in this reversal of educational systems.
The Spanish teachers had gone, along with the Spanish
Army. The Spanish friars who still remained were poorly

equipped to teach children the new facts of Philippine life. Filipino teachers were few. There were few Spanish textbooks, and none at all in the Filipino vernacular languages. Educational books were shipped directly from the United States, to be used to teach Filipino children their ABCs. Consequently, in the early years little Filipinos learned American history—about George Washington, Thomas Jefferson, and Abraham Lincoln, but nothing about José Rizal, Father Burgos, or Andres Bonifacio. The resulting confusion is illustrated by the classic Philippine story of the small boy asked to write a composition about "The Cow" (an unfamiliar beast in the land of the *carabao*). He wrote: "The cow gives milk, but as for me, give me liberty or give me death."

The textbook problem was eventually corrected, the dominance of the English language was unquestioned, and the task of bringing American style democracy to the Philippines was pursued with enthusiasm by all parties save one, the landowning *caciques,* who continued to speak Spanish and lift their noses at these Johnny-come-latelies, with their brash manners, giving Filipinos dangerous ideas about equality. But even this class was soon mollified, because the Americans did little to clip their wealth or their power over the peasants.

American teachers, civil servants, engineers arrived by the boatload. American experts, not always of the first rank, not all sober, but almost to a man dedicated to their exciting task, established a Bureau of Printing, a Bureau of Forestry, a Bureau of Fisheries, and the Customs Service. The Bureau

of Agriculture, Science and Mining set about with great success developing the natural resources of the islands.

Meanwhile, the U.S. Army was also at work, building
dams, bridges, and roads. The most spectacular accomplishment is the mountain Zigzag Road up from Manila to the
mountain resort of Baguio. This road did wonders for Philippine morale. Baguio recurs in Philippine history rather like
Versailles in French history. The pretty little town has a
fascination for well-to-do Filipinos because it is high, elegant, and above all, cool. It gives a statesman and a business-
man time and air to think, away from steaming, deafening
Manila. Sometimes, on the tops of trees at Baguio, one even
sees traces of frost, a sight of wonder in a country where one
can progress from the cradle to the grave without ever knowing what it feels like to be cool.

One area of Philippine society, however, proved itself to
be totally resistant to American charm and energy. That
area, predictably, was Moslem Mindanao, together with the
Sulu Archipelago. There the Americans found the same
obstinate hostility among the Moros as the Spaniards had
earlier. The *datus* refused to send their children to schools
in case the education opened the door to Christianity, and
they often sent the sons of their slaves in their places. For
years, Mindanao had to be left to the U.S. Army to adminis-
ter, which kept soldiers periodically locked in combat with
an ill-tempered, often fanatical guerrilla army that refused
to be intimidated by superior American fire power. A young
captain, John J. Pershing, distinguished himself in these
campaigns. Within the Moslem community was one particu-

larly fearsome sect, the Jura Mendattas, who according to military scuttlebutt, could not be stopped by bullets. When inflamed by drugs and religious frenzy, they continued to charge, waving their bolos, even when riddled. As recently as 1940, Gary Cooper and David Niven starred in a movie called "The Real Glory" about the U.S. Army fighting the Jura Mendattas.

As governor, William Howard Taft enjoyed considerable success, and developed a great love for the country. His combined American–Philippine administration redistributed certain Spanish church lands, and established limited self-government in the *barrios*. Taft left the Philippines in 1904 to become Secretary of War, while still maintaining authority over the territory, and in 1908, he became President. History being what it is, however, he is best remembered in the Philippines for the tremendous brick he dropped when, with the best intention in the world, he called the Filipinos "our little brown brothers." To this day, the expression will arouse Filipinos to paroxysms of rage or laughter, depending on who says it, how, and to whom.

In 1907, an elected national lower house took office, and Filipinos, who for centuries had lived under the rule of Spanish decree, never or rarely consulted about their own destiny, now began to discover the delights of the vote. At first this seemed likely to undercut the power of the landowners, but people of long-entrenched power have always learned to accommodate to new situations. They financed suitable, friendly political candidates, married their surplus daughters to promising young politicians, and not only re-

mained as powerful as ever, but added keen political blood
to the dilettante *ilustrado* tradition.

It was obvious to all educated observers that something
new and vibrant was happening to the formerly stagnant
Philippine life. The Filipinos were discovering themselves,
and beginning to see as a reality what Rizal had seen only
as an attainable ideal, that they were a "proud and sensitive"
people with one of the most exciting cultural heritages in all
Asia; a brave people, so stoic as to be almost incapable of
tears; hospitable to an overwhelming degree; able—given
sufficient self-confidence—to deal with any nation in the
world as intellectual equals. But that expression, "self-confidence," was the fly in the Philippine ointment, the perennial
doubt whether they would hold, if the crunch came. Out of
these stirrings of national awareness emerged several figures
of great political stature. Dr. Trinidad Tavera was the first.
Tavera died in 1925, at the age of sixty-eight. He was followed by Manuel Quezon, Sergio Osmeña, and others—men
who were to mold Philippine history and guide the nation
to independence.

The great American adventure in the Philippines has left
many legacies, most of them, one is happy to say, positive.
Some were brilliant, a few were appalling, many were
happy, others less happy. The Philippines is in some ways the
most fortunate of all Asian nations in that the Filipinos are
the pupils of not one but two magnificent cultures, vastly different, but complementary rather than conflicting. From
Spain they learned Christianity, civilization, courage, and

the importance of pride and human dignity. From the Americans they developed a passion for freedom and democracy. (The interruption of the democratic process by President Marcos's decree of martial law in September 1972, however it turns out, can only be an interlude.) They acquired a passion for politics and the dizzy, roller-coaster sensation of a completely free press. English replaced Spanish as the effective common language, with all the world-wide vigor the English language instills. At the same time, Spanish remained as the language of elegance and refinement. The love of politics has assumed both its Jekyll and its Hyde form in the Philippines in its devotion to idealism, progress, and equality at one end, with the golden possibilities of graft, corruption, and the pork barrel at the other end. The presidential palace of Malacañang, on the banks of the Pasig River in Manila, has invariably been inhabited by honest men, but some remarkable scalawags have prospered close by.

The American years also gave the Filipinos a deep love for the United States as an ideal, and for the Americans as people, for their loose-limbed informality and freedom from old European arrogance. The Tavera ambition is not dead. A strong minority group in the Philippines still dreams that the nation one day may follow that other Pacific civilization, Hawaii, into the American Union. Americans in the Philippines thought that their own way of life was the best, but they also wanted the Filipinos to share it to the full. This love that the Filipinos give America has been received in curious ways, of which the strongest is total indifference. It

takes a cataclysm to put the Philippines on the front pages
of American newspapers, and after the succession of sensational events in 1972, educated Filipinos may be excused for
wondering if they have exhausted their ration of interest on
the part of Americans for the next decade.

President Woodrow Wilson became President in 1912,
carrying the Democratic Party to power after sixteen years
of the opposition (the previous Democratic President had
been Grover Cleveland, whose term expired in 1896, two
years before the collapse of Spanish power in the Philippines). Until Wilson's election, the Democrats had noisily
opposed Republican "imperialism." Any ideas Wilson might
have nurtured of granting independence to the Philippines
ended with the outbreak of World War I in 1914. With matters more important on his mind, Wilson sought to "Filipinize" the islands by replacing American civil executives with
Filipinos. The result of this well-intentioned policy might
have been foreseen. The Filipinos were hopelessly unpre-
pared for the responsibility. It was conferred much too soon.
The effects of Spanish rule had not yet been shaken off. Men
as young as thirty could remember saluting the Spanish flag
in school. If the Americans insisted on Filipino executives,
where were they to be found? To that there was only one
answer: among the landowners, their children, and their
protégés. So, in advance, the Americans condemned themselves to fail where the Spaniards had failed, in land reform.
The landowners and their families would see to that.

The Filipinos were learning, nevertheless. They were taking to the political process with amazing confidence, learning how to play one American interest against another, to their own advantage. What changes were made, were made gradually, peacefully, and rarely with bitterness. Few feelings of inferiority were inculcated by the Americans into the Filipinos. The two peoples met and worked as equals. There was no color line. In almost all Anglo-Saxon Protestant imperial colonies, such as India and the African colonies, intermarriage was socially discouraged; not so in the Philippines. Many Americans married Filipinas, and while the majority moved on to the United States, a small but interesting admixture of American blood began to enhance the already beautiful Malay-Spanish-Chinese look possessed by many of the people.

This vitally important period of Philippine history is so amiable, so full of slow but consistent progress, mutual esteem and respect, that its history would have been positively boring, as boring as the history of modern Switzerland or Sweden, but for the occasionally colorful characters who emerge from it, and most notably Manuel Quezon, the father of Philippine independence.

Chapter 6

INDEPENDENCE—
SO NEAR AND YET . . .

MANUEL LUIS QUEZON Y MOLINA was born on August 19, 1878, the son of two schoolteachers, in the province of Tabayas, later to be renamed the province of Quezon. Like most important Filipinos, before and since, he graduated in the school of sudden death, but unlike many of his contemporaries his life did not end with a bullet or a bolo in the heart. He was twenty when he saw the Spanish flag hauled down for the last time over Manila Bay, and although he was already a young revolutionary, he confessed in his memoirs that he wept at the sight. The story is one more illustration of the dichotomy of *ilustrado* feeling at the end of the nineteenth century: the hunger for freedom combined with the love of Spanish grandeur—José Rizal volunteering to serve in the Spanish Army against the Americans, and Quezon weeping when the Spanish flag is lowered.

When Aguinaldo declared war on the United States, Quezon joined the Philippine forces and served as a guerrilla officer throughout the campaign. After Aguinaldo's capture and conversion, Quezon hung up his uniform and returned to Manila to resume his education, and was duly called to the Manila bar as a lawyer. He was a small, dynamically handsome man with Spanish rather than Malay features, crisp, thick hair and a disdainful expression. He was rarely seen without a cigarette between his fingers. Like most *ilustrados* he aimed at the higher ideals and was impatient of detail. Throughout his career he showed little real interest in improving the lot of the peasant, but in a larger political context he could sense where the interests of his country lay. In 1909, when he was only thirty-one, he was chosen by the Philippine Assembly as the Filipino Resident Commissioner in Washington, and made an impressive plea for independence before the House of Representatives.

For more than twenty years Quezon and Sergio Osmeña of Cebu dominated Philippine politics, sometimes working together, sometimes in adversary positions. In some respects their relationship paralleled that of Gladstone and Disraeli in Victorian England. If Osmeña was the more suave, and perhaps the more capable of the two, Quezon was the more dramatic and aggressive. In the early 1920s, Quezon tangled so violently with the American Governor-General of the Philippines, General Leonard S. Wood, that it seriously affected his own health, and may have hastened Wood's death in 1927. The conflict was so bitter that it made subsequent Governors-General, Henry L. Stimson, Dwight F. Davis,

Theodore Roosevelt, Jr., and Frank Murphy less willing to confront Quezon's combination of charm and wrath.

Wood was a soldier, a former Military Governor of Cuba, and an officer in charge of campaigns against the Moros. He had the military man's forthrightness, and was without diplomatic guile. Wood saw that Wilson's policy of Filipinization was actually slowing rather than hastening Philippine independence, and he made the politically unpopular decision of restoring Americans to responsible posts in the islands. This led Quezon to utter his famous cry from the heart: "I prefer a government run like hell by Filipinos to a government run like heaven by Americans"—subsequently the dictum of every leader against colonial rule.

The years 1934 and 1935 were decisive in Philippine history because they brought the country to within only a step of complete independence in all fields. In 1934, the formal terms of independence were spelled out in the Tydings-McDuffie Act which stated that the Philippines was to become a self-governing Commonwealth under the American flag until the year 1946 when total independence would be proclaimed. Elections were set for 1935, and every six years thereafter. The term of office was later reduced to four years.

The election of Quezon as first President of the Commonwealth of the Philippines, with Sergio Osmeña as his running mate, was a foregone conclusion. Quezon's official opponent was Bishop Gregorio Aglipay of the Filipino Independent Church. The great surprise came when Emilio Aguinaldo himself announced that he intended to come out of retirement and campaign for the presidency. There was no reason why he should not run. He was sixty-five, only eight years older than Quezon and Osmeña, who were the same age. But he already belonged ineluctably to the nation's past. That he pined for the old glory days in the field of battle against the Spaniards and the Americans is beyond doubt. Occasionally he had been fed small posts for his prestige value, and complained to visitors, "I am only a helper. Once I was President." Quezon won by 700,000 votes to Aguinaldo's 179,000 and Aglipay's 148,000, and Aguinaldo returned to his fortress-like home outside Manila muttering that he had been robbed, and would have been elected had the votes been fairly counted.

Despite the small number of eligible voters, the election was historic, in that a Filipino chief executive had been elected to the highest office in the land by the direct vote of the Philippine people. The election marked another triumph, less widely noticed, namely the triumph of the English language. Orators like Quezon and Osmeña, journalists like Carlos P. Romulo, scholars, and columnists used the English language as ably as any people in the world. The standard of the English-language newspapers in Manila was as high as, and frequently higher than, newspapers in many cities of the United States. Because the language was often uttered by the Filipinos in a slow, slightly singsong accent, as though they were speaking a second language with deliberation, rather than their own language, they often surprised American politicians into thinking they were dealing with innocents, and the Americans were consequently taken aback to find themselves outwitted both in dialectic and acumen by what they thought of as the smiling, untutored little Filipinos.

Quezon was now in command of a virtually independent nation, the Americans being largely cast in the role of advisers. His problems were huge because this was the period when the aggressive policies of Nazi Germany and Imperial Japan were reaching full momentum, and the Philippines stood in the direct path of Japan's expansion in Asia. To counter the Japanese threat, Quezon secured General Douglas MacArthur to raise a citizen Philippine Army. MacArthur's appointment was a major coup for Quezon. MacArthur was already America's most distinguished soldier. He was also the son of General Arthur MacArthur who had fought Aguinaldo in the Philippine-American war.

The other major problem was that which haunted every Philippine administration, be it Spanish, American, or Filipino—the problem of the peasant, multiplying endlessly, held by his debts to near-peonage; the helpless, practically illiterate tools of the landowners, the Church, and the Chinese moneylenders, with a per capita income of only a few dollars a year. Quezon went through the usual motions of coming to their aid. A few large, landed estates were purchased by the government and sold to the tenants on the installment plan, but, as usual, the assistance was a drop in the ocean to actual needs, every reform submerged by the appearance of new babies, the Philippines increase in population being one of the highest, per capita, in the world.

War began in Europe in September 1939. The United

States remained neutral. France fell to Hitler's fast Panzers in June 1940, and for a full year, Britain, battered by the Luftwaffe and the U-boats, stood alone against a continent of Europe conquered by the Germans, as she had done more than a century before against the Europe of Napoleon. Hitler carried his Napoleonic parallel further when he attacked the U.S.S.R. in June 1941. Within weeks the Germans were at the gates of Moscow and Leningrad, and German officers could see the towers of the Kremlin through their field glasses. Japan, stimulated by the triumphs of her German allies, swelled and swelled, growing steadily more malevolent, and poised to seize all Asia. The Japanese Army and Navy controlled the entire Chinese coastline. The Chinese Nationalist armies of Chiang Kai Shek, friendly to the United States and to the Philippines, had been driven inland to a temporary capital at Chungking. Above and around the Philippines, the sky and the seas were dark with Japanese menace.

This monstrous presence formed a frightening backdrop to the politics of the Philippines as they unfolded through 1940 and 1941. According to the original Constitution of the Philippine Commonwealth, the President was elected for one six-year term only, but accommodations could be made that would not, in American practice, be considered according to Hoyle. Quezon should have stood down in November 1941, but the Constitution was amended to enable him to run for a second term, which he did, winning easily, on November 11, 1941. Again Sergio Osmeña was his running mate, and the understanding between the two, not legally enforceable, was that Quezon would stand down after two years, and yield the presidency to Osmeña.

But events of world-shattering importance were literally a matter of days away. On December 7, less than one month after Quezon's re-election, the Japanese bombed Pearl Harbor, and the Philippines, the unconsidered and innocent bystander on the world scene, was plunged into a war which would devastate it more thoroughly than any other Allied country on earth.

Chapter 7

THE MASSACRE OF A NATION

THE PACIFIC CAMPAIGN of World War II, beginning with Pearl Harbor and ending with the surrender of the Japanese on August 14, 1945, ranged throughout Asia to the borders of Australia and India. For a year the Japanese triumphed everywhere; no target seemed beyond the reach of their swarming tentacles. They destroyed the fleets of the United States, Britain, and the Netherlands, occupied the Dutch Indonesian empire, captured the supposedly impregnable British fortress of Singapore, sank the *Prince of Wales* and the *Repulse,* the world's two greatest battleships, in a matter of minutes, for the loss of only a couple of planes.

Despite these horrendous defeats, the United States decided to concentrate its main effort on the destruction of Nazi Germany first and Japan afterward. From the beginning almost to the end, the Pacific campaign was a holding operation, reinforced by a brilliant tactic of island hopping.

Yet, with one exception, the Pacific war did little material damage to the Allied countries. That exception was the Philippines. By the end of the war, as mentioned earlier, Manila was the most devastated city in the world after Warsaw. And other Philippine cities were little better off.

The war began for the Philippines just one week after Pearl Harbor, on December 15, when most of its people were asleep. Until then, despite the alarming news pouring out of their radios and newspapers, the Filipinos felt they had no reason to fear for themselves and their homes and families. General Douglas MacArthur, a soldier revered throughout the country, had been in charge of Philippine defenses since the inauguration of the Commonwealth in 1935, and had assured the Filipinos that they were protected against all enemies. MacArthur had an almost mystic feeling for both dynasty and history. His father had brought American civilization to the Philippines, and it was only natural that his own mission was to preserve it. However controversial MacArthur's personality was in his own country, he was considered by those who should know best— namely the Filipinos—to be the man who, above all others, understood the Filipino soul.

President Quezon was in his summer residence in Baguio, and was awakened by his secretary with the news that bombs were falling on the Philippines, some not far from Baguio itself.

Quezon rose and ordered his entourage immediately back to Manila by car, a decision that did not reflect the best judgment on his part as the only road was by the magnificent, but easily pin-pointed Zigzag Road built by the U.S. Army, laced with hairpin bends, and painted white.

As the presidential convoy drove through the mountains of Luzon they saw seventeen planes flying in V formation, and cheered, believing them to be American. A few minutes later, the sound of explosions rocked their composure. Here they were, dangerously exposed, their breakfasts as yet undigested, and already the Philippines was under attack. Progress was slow, the cities of San Fernando and Angeles clogged with traffic, civilian and military, paralyzed by the bombardments and the general confusion. The U.S. Army camp at Angeles was blazing, and all logic had disappeared from the scene as it unfolded itself before the horrified presidential party. In Quezon City, for example, they were told that a constable on traffic duty had pulled his gun and fired at a low-flying Japanese fighter. The fighter had wheeled, returned, and machine-gunned him to death.

In Manila, the news was confusing, contradictory except that it was all bad. With the U.S. Navy destroyed at Pearl Harbor, the Japanese ground troops had had no difficulty landing at Lingayen Gulf, Lamon Bay, and elsewhere on Luzon Island. The U.S. Air Force had not risen to resist them because all the planes had been destroyed at Clark Field. The Philippines was helpless to prevent invasion. MacArthur's original plan to defend the Philippines "on the beaches" had to be hastily abandoned, and the American–Philippine forces were ordered back into the interior.

MacArthur gave Quezon the grave news that Manila

would have to be abandoned to the Japanese, and that his forces would be grouped to fight from stronger positions on the bastion peninsula of Bataan which protects Manila Bay. General MacArthur's declaration of Manila as an "open city" was one of the tragic ironies of the war. To begin with it created a painful impact of defeatism on an Allied world which had become conditioned to the heroic defenses of cities like London and Leningrad. And in the end it did not save the beautiful city of Manila from being bombed and shelled into rubble.

It was scarcely surprising that Quezon too was caught up in the general panic, and considered withdrawing from the war and declaring the Philippines neutral, with a personal appeal to the Japanese Emperor. Quezon's health was poor, and there was much sympathy for his agony as he saw the country he had largely created disintegrating before his eyes, but other members of his Cabinet persuaded him to withdraw from Manila to the fortress island of Corregidor and continue the fight.

Before he left, Quezon took aside several senior Philippine officials whose thankless task was to stay behind and face the Japanese conquerors. Jorge B. Vargas, the colorful mayor of Manila, was one of the officials. He had perhaps the most difficult job of all, to hold the great city together. One man who insisted on staying despite Quezon's pleas to accompany him was the Chief Justice of the Supreme Court, José Abad Santos. Abad Santos, a man of unswerving religious faith, insisted that his duty was to remain at his post.

Sadly, silently, the government of the Philippines quit

Manila, leaving it to the mercy of a conqueror whose ruthless behavior and blood lust had spread terror throughout
Asia. Shortly after the Filipinos and the Americans had
gone, the Japanese arrived, behind their flag of the Rising
Sun, and their appearance was just as shocking as the Filipinos had expected. For forty years, Filipinos had been accustomed to tall, rangy, cheerful Americans chewing gum
and giving candy to children. The Japanese were small,
dragging swords that seemed too big for them, their shirt
collars open, over stiff, uncomfortable uniforms. They wore
absurd, tall, peaked caps. Many were bespectacled and
pedaled bicycles. And yet they had conquered three mighty
empires in a matter of weeks, and they were the lords of
all Asia.

Quezon's flight was a terrible one for a sick man. He
stayed only a few days on Corregidor, which was preparing
itself for attack. On February 20, 1942, he left Corregidor
by submarine for the island of Panay to the south. From
Panay he went to Negros, thence to Mindanao, thence to
Australia, and finally he flew to Washington, D.C. where
he was greeted personally by President Roosevelt.

The flight of Quezon and the occupation of Manila were
a preliminary to the long, fearful Battle of Bataan. As one
can see on the map, Bataan is a strip of land running down
the other side of Manila Bay from the capital. From Dewey
Boulevard, Manila's principal avenue, it can be clearly seen
on the horizon, as can the island of Corregidor.

Contingency plans drawn up before the war had already
envisaged the possibility of the American and Philippine

forces being obliged to defend Bataan. It was conceived
then as a holding action, while reinforcements were brought
up. The experts did not believe that it could be held on its
own. A prolonged battle, they said, would end in exhaustion
and defeat. But General MacArthur was an optimist, and a
great admirer of Marshal Foch, the French commander in
World War I, and Foch's policy of *"L'attaque! L'attaque!
Toujours l'attaque!"* (at the cost of countless million lives).
But two of the premises on which MacArthur had counted
had ceased to exist. The protection he had expected from
the U.S. Air Force disappeared when the Air Force was
destroyed at Clark Field. And much of the vast supply of rice
and flour stockpiled for the battle had been left behind in
the pellmell withdrawal to the peninsula, and had fallen
into Japanese hands.

To make the food situation more critical, thousands of
Philippine citizens had fled with the army into the peninsula, crowding into army camps, obstructing military movements, eating the food. The battle lasted from December 9,
1941 until April 9, 1942, a series of desperate stands and
strategic retreats. The Filipino troops trained by MacArthur
fought heroically, even though relations between them and
the American soldiers steadily worsened. All the horses and
mules were killed and eaten. The rains for which the troops
prayed did not come, and they collapsed of thirst, starvation,
and disease. There was also a weird propaganda war by
radio across Manila Bay. From Corregidor, the expression
of the Philippine determination to resist was broadcast in
the voice of General Carlos P. Romulo, a flamboyant journalist and newspaper proprietor, now military spokesman for

General MacArthur in the Philippines. From Manila came a voice out of the past urging the Filipinos to lay down their arms and save themselves from inevitable slaughter. President Emilio Aguinaldo, recruited by Japanese propagandists, was speaking to his countrymen.

In February, President Roosevelt ordered General MacArthur to leave the Philippines altogether and move to Australia to assume command of the newly designated Southwest Pacific Area. Filipinos everywhere heard the news with despair. This, they felt, was the end, even though MacArthur did his characteristic best to identify himself with the nation's fortunes. He uttered his famous rallying call, "I will return," but everybody asked "When?"

With MacArthur gone, the disintegration of the American–Philippine resistance accelerated. The Filipinos complained that the Americans would not share their food with them, or even bathe in the same water. Philippine officers were often placed under the orders of American officers of much lower rank, majors given orders by lieutenants, and the like.

By the beginning of April, the Americans and Filipinos held only a small ring at the tip of Bataan, their position hopeless, their morale in shreds. They had heard stories, often depressingly true, of Japanese massacring their prisoners, and believed that they were about to share the same fate. From Australia, MacArthur ordered the American commander, General Jonathan Wainwright, to make one last charge, a hopelessly romantic order, which once again echoed Marshal Foch who said, *"Mon centre cède, ma flanc droite et ma flanc gauche recule. Situation excellente. J'at-*

taque." ("My center is giving way, my right and left flanks
are withdrawing. Situation excellent. I attack!") Some hours
later, on April 9, Bataan fell, and 78,000 American and
Philippine troops surrendered to the Japanese.

But their ordeal had only begun. Starving, riddled with
dysentery, their wounds turning gangrenous, they began the
notorious "Death March" to the distant prison camps at
Capas and O'Donnell. Clubs and bayonets drove them
through the *barrios*. The march, under the eyes of the peasants, was intended by the Japanese as a final humiliation of
the Americans, and the ultimate glorification of the Asian
Japanese.

All that now remained on Luzon was the fortress of Corregidor. Although its underground fortifications were impressive, with interlocking tunnels and massive howitzers,
it was in little better shape than the mainland for food,
water, and ammunition, and it was shelled and bombed into
surrender after a siege of twenty-seven days. The Japanese
victory in the Philippines was complete, except for mopping-
up operations. But some comfort could be taken from the
fact that the Japanese had been forced seriously behind
schedule, and the port of Manila had been completely closed
to them for six vital months.

One turns now from the tragedy of millions to the martyrdom of one man, Chief Justice Abad Santos, who had elected
to remain behind at his post rather than follow Manuel
Quezon into exile.

Abad Santos was sixty-six years old. He had had a distinguished law career in both the United States and the Philippines before his appointment to the Supreme Court shortly before the war. As soon as the Japanese arrived, he was summoned to the commandant's office and ordered to renounce his oath of allegiance to the United States. He refused. On May 2, 1942, while the guns were still firing on Corregidor, he was summoned by a Japanese interpreter to the Japanese headquarters, a schoolhouse in Malabang, Lanao. His son, José Jr., one of his five children, waited outside. Leaving after a few minutes, he said to his son with a kind of incredulous smile as though he could not believe his ears, "I have been condemned to be executed." The son burst into tears. Abad Santos put his arm around the young man's shoulder, and said, "Don't cry. What is the matter with you? Show these people"—indicating the Japanese guards standing around—"that you are brave. It is a rare opportunity to die for one's country, and not everybody is given that chance."

A few minutes later he was dead. The Chief Justice of the Supreme Court of the Philippines went to his death defending the honor of the United States. That his name is completely unknown in the United States except by specialist scholars, and that his memory has never been honored by so much as a postage stamp is another example of the lack of American interest in a country that has given so much love to America.

Another figure now makes his appearance, or rather reappearance in the conquered Philippines. All wars throw up odd, forgotten, sometimes lustrous survivors from past history. General Artemio Ricarte turned up unexpectedly from Tokyo. Ricarte had been one of Aguinaldo's favorite generals in the war against the Americans. The exploit for which he was best known to Filipino schoolchildren occurred on June 10, 1941 when he had led 3,000 badly armed Filipinos against 4,000 Americans, and put them to rout. He had later moved to Japan rather than take an oath of allegiance to the United States. There he lived in semi-starvation, worked as an odd-job man, taught Spanish in a Tokyo school for which he earned a few dollars a month. To help survive, Mrs. Ricarte ran a restaurant, mostly for Filipinos passing through Japan, specializing in Philippine dishes like *adobo* and *sinigang*. Customers would leave a cash donation on top of the check for the penniless, exiled patriot.

Suddenly, Ricarte was back in the Philippines, for the first time in forty years. He made his first call on his old boss, General Aguinaldo, now seventy-three, and invited Aguinaldo to rally to the Japanese, and lend the prestige of his name to the anti-American crusade in Asia. Ricarte wore a Japanese uniform and a Samurai sword. According to Aguinaldo in his memoirs, Ricarte bullied him, and made it plain that the Japanese would tolerate no evasions. Those who were not for Japan were against her. He boasted that he himself was to be appointed head of the new Philippine government which was to be installed by the Japanese. He brandished his sword, a gift, he said, from Premier Tojo of Japan with which, he said, "I will cut the American chain off my dear Motherland."

"I looked at him," Aguinaldo recalled, "with a mixture
of pity and contempt. How he must have regretted living
away from so much economic and cultural progress in his
own country, under the American flag. Much of it must have
been still evident (even to him), in spite of the paralyzation
of normal activities under Japanese rule."

Nevertheless, Aguinaldo had himself been broadcasting for
the Japanese.

Ricarte's melodramatic return was a part of Japan's longer-
term strategy for the Philippines. It was clear to them that
something had to be offered to the people to compensate for
what they had lost. Although the country was still comparatively quiet, and had not yet erupted into the nation-
wide guerrilla warfare which would soon tear the nation to
shreds, the fact was that the Philippine people were dying—
trite and almost incredible though it may sound—of broken
hearts. They pined for their new Commonwealth, the Americans, for Manuel Quezon, for General MacArthur. Psycho-
logically, as well as physically, they were wasting away.
Their sufferings were aggravated by the simple stupidity of
the Japanese who sometimes deliberately, but often through
ignorance, did the wrong things in small matters which
make so much difference to the human soul. Lord Chesterfield (1694–1773) said that it was an error of historians to
attribute mighty events to important causes. The opposite is
often true, and Chesterfield's aphorism is repeated in different words by David Everett who lived a century later, and
wrote:

Large streams from little fountains flow,
Tall oaks from little acorns grow.

The Japanese seized chickens and pigs without payment. They bathed naked in the streets, indifferent to the shock this caused to Philippine modesty. They showed a hopeless lack of understanding of the Philippine respect for age and seniority, and slapped distinguished gentlemen who failed to salute them.

In 1943, Filipinos were horrified to see German officers strolling through Manila. They had been flown from Tokyo to inspect fortifications and tour the prison camps. These were white men condoning the horrors of Japanese occupation and the atrocities of the prisoner-of-war camps. The sight of the heel-clicking Germans only made Filipinos more homesick than ever for the Americans.

After the fall of Bataan, the Japanese in their own usually clumsy way sought to win over the Filipinos from their attachment to the United States. They released Filipino prisoners-of-war as a gesture of friendship. They incorporated the islands into a "Greater Asia Co-Prosperity Sphere" of economic co-operation.

Certain elements within the Philippines had rallied to their support to some extent. Among them were members of the pre-war Ganap Party which had been openly pro-Japanese. Some of the aristocratic, Spanish-speaking *cacique* families hoped for an Axis victory. They were not so much pro-Japanese as pro-Spanish, and, by transference, pro-German. They still looked to Spain as their cultural motherland, considered the Americans superficial *arrivistes* on the

Philippine scene; and the Fascist government of General Franco in Spain was a treaty ally of Hitler. Too much must not be made of this, nor can too many generalizations be made. Other Spanish-Filipino families were even more emphatically on the side of the Americans and, incredibly in such a period as this, were still able to withdraw to the Wack Wack Golf Club and play golf rather than co-operate with the conquerors.

On October 14, 1943, while the Americans were counterattacking from island to island in the Pacific, a Japanese-sponsored Philippine government took office. It called itself the Second Republic, after the First Republic formed by General Aguinaldo in 1898. The appointed President was José P. Laurel, one of the Philippines's most distinguished lawyers. Laurel had asked to accompany Quezon into exile, but had been ordered to remain behind to try to ameliorate the lot of the people. The Japanese had placed him in charge of law and order, and only a few months earlier he had been shot by someone unknown at the Wack Wack Golf Club because of the pro-Japanese sentiments ascribed to him.

The ceremony inaugurating the new government was opened by Jorge B. Vargas, mayor of Manila, who announced to a cheering crowd that the Japanese were withdrawing their military administration. General Aguinaldo took part in the ceremony side by side with Artemio Ricarte, and saw the same Philippine flag raised that they themselves had raised nearly half a century earlier. A twenty-one-gun Japanese salute preceded Laurel's inaugural speech. The speech itself crowned the many ironies by being delivered in English. Laurel described "the momentous occasion" and said, "As we witness the triumphal realization of our national ideal, we would be sadly wanting in those magnanimous qualities . . . if we did not forgive the wounds and havoc inflicted by the war, the immolation of our youth with their golden promises of the future, the untold sufferings undergone by our innocent population." It was, according to observers, an occasion of high emotion, and President Laurel resumed extemporaneously in Tagalog with an exhortation, in effect, for Filipinos to keep their chins up.

The parallel between Laurel's puppet government in Manila, and Marshal Pétain's puppet government in German-occupied France, cannot be taken too far. Pétain was totally committed to collaboration. In the Philippines many of the men most inflexibly committed to the defeat of the Japanese actually joined Laurel's Cabinet. The most prominent was Manuel Roxas, who as a Brigadier General had been captured in Mindanao, released, and appointed to the Cabinet as Chairman of the Economic Planning Board, without ever ceasing to lead the Philippine resistance movement from his own office.

The Japanese authorities were most certainly hoping for a trouble-free solution, along Pétainist lines, to the Philippine problem, and they were quickly disillusioned. Taking advantage of the proclamation of independence and proclaiming sovereignty for the new republic, Filipino leaders began protesting against Japanese military practices. They protested against the impressing of young Filipinos into the

Japanese Army, and demanded the release of those already serving. They protested against the forcible acquisition of private houses for Japanese military personnel. Guerrillas, released from prison under amnesty, immediately took to the hills to resume the fight. In the mild words of Senator Claro M. Rector in later years, "legal and technical difficulties were placed in the path of Japan's system of control." Or, in other words, the westernized Japanese no less than the West itself, could find themselves baffled by the inscrutable workings of the Oriental mind.

As the war slowly turned against the Japanese, the resistance spread and Japanese oppression became more ruthless. Brilliant resistance fighters emerged, as tough and wiry as the Japanese themselves. One of them was a certain young, handsome fellow, a lawyer in peacetime, named Ferdinand Marcos, another subsequent President of the Philippines.

The Filipinos harassed and sabotaged the Japanese, and supplied the American intelligence forces overseas with streams of information about Japanese military dispositions. By such acts, the Filipinos were learning a sensation they had never known before in their often tragic history, the sensation of hate. They hated the Japanese, and, even worse, they began slowly to hate one another. Guerrilla chieftains fought each other as mercilessly as they fought the Japanese. They settled old scores and feuds, eliminated potential postwar business rivals and political opponents.

In the middle of this orgy of hate, torture, and death, the Filipinos received further appalling news. On August 1, 1944, President Manuel Quezon died in the United States at the age of sixty-six. He had just finished his memoirs, *The Good Fight,* but never lived to see their publication. The shock to the Filipinos was as great as, or greater than, the shock felt in the United States nine months later with the death of President Roosevelt. The Americans at least had the power to rise from their sense of shock. They were on the threshold of the greatest victory in military history. The Filipinos were prostrate under a conqueror. Far away, in Washington, D.C., a new President of the Commonwealth was proclaimed, Sergio Osmeña. Closer to home, the President of the Second Republic, José Laurel, still sought desperately to act as a buffer between the Japanese and the Filipinos. And all the while the forces of General MacArthur were coming closer and closer. The great battle to the death for the Philippines was about to begin.

Chapter 8

A MILLION DEAD FILIPINOS

On January 9, 1945, the U.S. Navy, suffering heavy casualties as they sailed through mists of kamikaze suicide planes, put troops ashore at Lingayen in Luzon. Declaring, "I have returned," General MacArthur trod through the surf to the shore, providing one of the most famous photographs of the war. The citizens of Lingayen, the capital of the province of Pangasinan, who had cowered in shelters for days under the annihilating naval bombardments, emerged to greet their liberators, and found themselves face to face with Americans different from any they had ever known before. More than mere liberators, they appeared to be completely different human beings, harder than the friendly Yanks they remembered, the Yanks who now had rotted in prison camps for three years, and they wore different and more purposeful uniforms. The difference was almost symbolized by the new ear-hugging helmet, replacing the old trench helmet, dating from World War I, which had become identified in the Philippine mind with Bataan, Corregidor, and defeat. The planes overhead were different, and following hard on the heels of the first landings, came thousands of jeeps, trucks, tanks, communications equipment, and above all, mountains of K rations.

An incident took place almost at once, a tiny sparkle of human warmth in the ocean of wartime horror, and one that helps to explain the magical hold Douglas MacArthur had on the Philippine imagination. A Filipino youth burst through the guards to the nearest communications unit, and said, "My name is Perfecto Castro, and I want to talk to General MacArthur."

The American communications officer explained the difficulties in the way of granting such a request, adding that in four years of combat he himself had never set eyes on the General. The General, he added, was a quite busy man. The boy said that before the war he worked in the General's household. A call was put through to Command headquarters, and to the astonishment of all the GIs present, a jeep arrived, carrying the General's pennant, and the boy was taken to MacArthur who hugged him emotionally. Perfecto was given a GI uniform, the rank of sergeant, and he was attached to MacArthur's staff from then on.

MacArthur had returned, but seven months of the bloodiest fighting of the entire Asian war lay ahead for the people of the Philippines. Only one word—utter—can describe the Japanese resistance.

The soldiers of the opposing sides, locked in combat, trampled over the dazed and shell-shocked Filipino population, slaughtering them by the thousand. It is impossible for someone who was not present to grasp the intensity of the sufferings of Filipino men, women, and children. Not a single Filipino in those days could count his life expectancy in more than hours, often minutes. Not a child lived who had not seen dead bodies, or did not have a close relation who had been killed, maimed, or missing. Seize any Filipino over thirty-five at random, as the author has done, and ask him, "Do you remember the war?" And you will get answers like: "My name is Henry Garcia. I was ten, a runner for the guerrillas. We had a house on Lourdes Drive in San Juan, Rizal. The Japanese general who lived with us gave us chocolates, but my mother would not let me eat them because she feared they had been poisoned. One day, in 1942, an American flier landed by parachute in the middle of the marketplace. The Japanese took him and brought him to the general. I watched him come in. They ran a bayonet through him. Oh yes, and my uncle, Colonel Diokno, was on the Bataan Death March . . ."

Fighting as guerrillas were no fewer than five men of varying ages who, had they been killed, would have deprived the nation of five future Presidents of the Republic. Two other future Presidents, civilians in the war, escaped death from artillery fragments by inches. Flying shrapnel spattered around a newly born baby called Gemma Cruz who grew up to become "Miss International" of 1965. No one was spared the terror. This was "normal living" in the Phil-

ippines. The Filipinos had become, in the enduring phrase
of William Copeland, "a nation of survivors."

As has already been seen, even in this short book, what a
Filipino learns is not so much absorbed as sustained, not
quite a foreign body, but rather a self-nourishing entity
inside his consciousness. The peaceful "little brown brother"
of President McKinley still lives, and is encountered wherever one meets Filipinos, from cocktail parties to cockfights,
but he is a Dr. Jekyll within whom is another Filipino, his
alter ego, who is ruthless, independent, a survivor and, if
necessary, a killer. One of the most law-abiding peoples on
earth has become one of the most lawless.

The Japanese, in the three years they had ruled the Philippines, had grown increasingly frustrated by their inability to
understand how Malays, devout Catholics, could prefer
white Americans and their Protestant way of life to fellow-
Asians. Now that defeat was inevitable, the Japanese un-
leashed on them the full fury of their frustration. They
burned down villages and massacred entire populations.
They destroyed schools, churches, public buildings, farms,
harbor installations. They killed the *carabaos,* the domesti-
cated water buffaloes on which the Filipino farmer de-
pended absolutely for the tilling of his fields.

Death struck wholesale and without selectivity. Filipinos
died without knowing why they died. José Celeste, Vice-
Minister of Economic Affairs, died protesting, "But I am a
Vice-Minister." With him died his wife and family.

Fort Santiago Prison filled up and became a place of horror. Filipinos were tortured and then mutilated by the hun-

dreds. The Filipino people were being abused and humili-
ated on a scale unequaled by any national people involved
in the war. Even the Russians were not as cruelly used by
the Germans as the Filipinos were by the Japanese.

Not least, the Japanese High Command resolved to fight,
house by house, for the beautiful city of Manila, once called
"The Pearl of the Orient." Twenty thousand crack Japanese
troops entrenched themselves in the city. From January 9
to February 5, 1945, the Japanese busied themselves turning
the capital into a fortress. Firing positions were established
in every building and at every corner, especially inside the
Intramuros district. The streets were mined and barricaded,
and these, in turn, were covered by fire from antitank guns
and automatic weapons. Artillery pieces were placed in the
upper stories of some of the city's finest buildings.

This was tragedy in all its most majestic irony. Manila had
been such a tranquil, charming place; it had never thought
of war before. Three years earlier, when the Japanese in-
vaded, it had declared itself an open city, an act that was
greeted with bitter derision in such battered capitals as London and Moscow. Paris had also declared herself an open
city in 1940, and what good had it done France? The Russians had been openly contemptuous. Solomon Lozovsky,
the Moscow radio broadcaster, compared the timid attitude
of the Manilans to a "ladybug, who defends herself against
her enemies by lying on her back, and saying to her enemies,
'Please don't attack me. See how defenseless I am.'"

On February 7, the battle was joined. The American 37th
Division made an assault crossing of the Pasig River near

the presidential palace after a preliminary artillery bombardment. The following day it had penetrated to the Intramuros district where it was stopped by furious Japanese resistance.

In the meantime, the 1st Cavalry Division had wiped out all organized resistance north of the Pasig River. On February 11 it advanced rapidly southeast and reached Manila Bay near the pre-war Polo Club. On February 16, the 37th Division reached the eastern edge of Intramuros, and the 1st Cavalry was blasting its way north, foot by foot up Dewey Boulevard against increasingly stiff resistance. Artillery on both sides reduced the buildings along the Boulevard to rubble.

From February 18 to 22, the American and Filipino troops continued to close in on enemy forces holed up for a last stand in Intramuros and the port area that included the city's spectacular waterfront. In house-to-house fighting, the Americans captured, in turn, the High Commissioner's residence, the Elks Club, and the Army-Navy Club. From there troops of the 1st Cavalry managed to fight their way across the open square between the Army-Navy Club and the Manila Hotel, and broke into the lobby. They then fought their way up from the mezzanine to the top floor until the last Japanese in the building was dead.

For some days more, the Japanese forces continued to hold out in the Finance Building and in Fort Santiago. It was grim justice that so many Japanese died in that horrible tomb of so many Filipino patriots. Both American and Japanese guns were trained on the historic old Cathedral of San

Augustin, and hand-to-hand fighting went on inside its quadrangle. When it was cleared of Japanese, the bodies were found of six hundred Manilans and priests who had sought refuge there and died from machine-gun and artillery fire. They were not massacred. They had merely got in the way of the soldiers.

The guns were still firing when President Osmeña was driven to the windowless and pockmarked Palace of Malacañang. Even as he was giving orders to his staff, American troops found two Japanese entrenched in the palace grounds and killed them.

When silence fell, all that could be seen in every direction were ruins piled on ruins. The world-famous sunset which, every evening of his life, gives the Manileño an ever-changing riot of color, was hidden behind palls of black smoke, from which scarlet flame erupted like hemorrhages. That the population had survived even in the cellars was a miracle.

One of the facts of war is that it is a great crosser of t's and dotter of i's, and there are always loose ends to be tied. What, to begin with, happened to José Laurel and his Second Republic?

As early as September 1944, he had declared war on the United States and Great Britain, on the orders of the Japanese High Command. He rendered the declaration meaningless by declaring that there would be no conscription inasmuch as "the flower of Filipino youth has already been sacrificed on the battlefields of Bataan and Corregidor."

The Japanese then made the same mistake with Laurel

that the Germans made with Marshal Pétain. Both Pétain
and Laurel could make serious claims to legitimacy, and
maintain that their governments were constitutionally
formed. Had they been allowed to remain behind they
could have seriously tangled the situation for General de
Gaulle arriving in Paris with his self-appointed government, and for President Sergio Osmeña whose government
had been in exile for three years. As it was, the Germans
and the Japanese simplified matters for the leaders who had
sided with the Allies, and destroyed the prospects of the
leaders that they themselves had favored. The Japanese, seeing that the situation in the Philippines was hopeless, flew
Laurel to Tokyo, where he remained a prisoner until the
end of the war.

In the jungles and the remoter islands of the Philippines,
the war took a long time to wind up. Thousands of Japanese remained active, refusing to surrender (one was killed
as recently as 1972, leaving a comrade still carrying on the
fight even to the moment of writing). One man left behind
for the second time in his life, amid the flotsam and jetsam of
defeat, was General Artemio Ricarte. Ricarte's ending was
sad, but far from dishonorable. When the Americans retook
Manila, he retreated to the mountains even as he had done
forty-three years earlier escaping from the same enemy, the
Americans, but this time with the remnants of the Japanese.
He was never heard of again. He was an old man, and is
believed to have perished in the wilds of Northern Luzon
with a handful of other Filipinos who had chosen to collaborate with the Japanese to the end. For Ricarte it could be

said that he was true to his principles and never wavered. He fought the Americans all his life, and died as he would have wished, still fighting, a gun in his hand, in some unknown corner of his native land.

As for Emilio Aguinaldo, he just went home. He was accused of collaboration, but was never tried. He said later, of his broadcasts to the defenders of Bataan in 1942, "I was just remembering the fight I led. I saw my own soldiers die without affecting future events. To me that seemed to be what was happening on Bataan, and it seemed like the right thing to do." He was formally cleared at an amnesty in 1948.

The hangover from the delirium of victory was predictably bitter. Government bureaus with all their files had been destroyed. The U.S. Army tried to sort things out, and decide who had resisted and who had collaborated, but it was an almost impossible task. Partly because of the absence or destruction of official records, the army badly bungled the awards and payments to the Filipinos who had fought the Japanese, often without ceasing, since Bataan. Emerging from the jungles and scrambling down the mountains, carrying their weapons, they frequently discovered to their rage that they had arrived weeks, or even months too late, and the medals and the money were gone, awarded to smooth-talking individuals on the spot in Manila, who had been the first to catch the ear of the understandably confused U.S. Army paymasters and staff officers. The problem of the inequity and inadequacy of the payments and awards has never been solved, and continues to embitter Philippine–American relationships.

"Fair play for the guerrillas" became an obvious political campaign slogan, and no one was better qualified to make it his own than Ferdinand Marcos. Marcos at this time was twenty-seven years old, and had become the nation's leading military hero. The future President of the Philippines was already a man of formidable determination and ambition. He was born in Sarrat, a rural town of Ilocos Norte in west Luzon. Mariano Marcos, his father, a reasonably wealthy politician, was a stern disciplinarian. His advice to his four children—a small family by Philippine standards—was, "Don't start a fight until you know you can win it." By the age of eighteen, Ferdinand was an expert pistol and rifle shot, and at sixteen won the national championships in small-bore competition.

In 1935 he was accused of murder. The case was a sensation in the Philippines at the time. The accusation said that he murdered a politician who had insulted his father. He was not arrested until 1939, when he was within five months of graduating from law school, and while out on bail, won the bar examinations with the highest average in Philippine history, 98.01 percent. When the judges at his trial, understandably sardonic, accused him of cheating, he suggested they give him an oral examination. They did so and he scored 92.35 percent, the second highest average in the country's history. It is scarcely surprising that he pleaded his own case before the Supreme Court, and even less surprising that he was exonerated on a technicality, on the grounds of conflicting evidence. But the charge of murder plagued him for the rest of his career.

His war career was fantastic. A natural fighter, he won the first of his two U.S. Silver Stars on Bataan, and a few weeks later, while the battle was still going on, he was recommended for the U.S. Medal of Honor. But the recommendation, although on record, was never filed. Had it been filed, Marcos would have become the only Filipino in history to win America's highest military honor. Badly wounded by shrapnel fragments and rifle fire, he nevertheless endured the Death March to Camp O'Donnell. There he was tortured by the Japanese Secret Police until he agreed to reveal to the Japanese the whereabouts of a Filipino guerrilla camp. He led them into an ambush which wiped them out, and escaped into the hills. He was wounded twice more, won a second Silver Star, and finished the war the most decorated soldier in the Philippines.

After the war, he turned his formidable energy and ruthlessness in the direction of politics. The injustices of the war payments became a political handle he could legitimately make his own. He claimed that he himself had been cheated of both pay and decorations. As the scion of an *ilustrado* family he could largely ignore the personal financial losses, which made his stand all the stronger as the spokesman for the rest. There was no doubt even now of the ambitions of this handsome, slim-hipped, dynamic young man: he was seeing Malacañang as his future home.

Chapter 9

THE SURVIVORS

"Iam seges est ubi fuit" ("Now corn grows where Troy was")—Aeneas in *Virgil*.

MANILA WAS NOT the only city left a ruin by the Japanese. Cebu City, the second largest city in the country, was also in ashes. Baguio, the summer capital, had been bombed to rubble. Such was the reality of what, at the beginning of this book, had been a mere statistic. By the time the country was finally free of the Japanese, nearly a million Filipinos were dead out of a population of 20 million, losses greater than those of the United States, Britain, and France combined. It is almost impossible to exaggerate the extent of such staggering losses, the bulk having been sustained by the country's young men.

No country on earth at this time needed a motherland's protection more than the Philippines needed the United States. The protection would have been willingly forthcoming, but for the fact that a symbolic date was approaching.

The United States had sworn to give the Philippines independence on July 4, 1946. It had been a magical date ever since 1934 when it entered the statute books with the Tydings-McDuffie Act. All logic cried out that the date should be put off until the prostrate country had made at least some progress toward recovery. But logic had no place among such emotional forces. Pre-war Philippine politics, directed by Quezon and President Osmeña was wholly committed to independence by that date. Washington, for its part, wanted to demonstrate to its imperialist Allies, Britain and France, how it should be done, how empires can be shed with dignity. And, in the long run, the American kill-or-cure politics of letting the Philippines stand on its own feet proved right, although the patient was all but on the deathbed before the long, slow, and far from complete recovery began.

The problems facing the baby republic almost defied imagination. Its exchequer was at zero. The Japanese and the guerrillas had killed, stolen, and eaten the *carabaos,* which were essential for Philippine farming. They had also been compelled to eat the green seed which should have been planted. Rice mills, warehouses, and inter-island shipping were destroyed, and most of the harbors were blocked by wreckage. Manila Bay was a pathetic sight, choked with rusting hulks sticking out of the water. The untended cane fields were deep in weeds. The vital hemp industry was in ruins. The coconut plantations had largely survived, but there was no way to take the product to the markets because all the transportation had been destroyed. Even apart from the million dead, the surviving men, able-bodied only by

name, were weak from malnutrition. Malaria, which had
been eradicated by the United States Army before the war,
had returned in a virulent form to infest the entire population.

Nevertheless, public opinion on both sides of the Pacific
demanded independence for the Philippines on the promised
date, and it is relevant at this point to examine briefly the
Philippine political system. The Constitution was modeled
closely on that of the United States, with an executive, a
legislature, and a judiciary, fulfilling similar functions to
those of the United States. The Philippines Constitution
even anticipated the amendment to the American Constitution limiting the presidency to two four-year terms. There
were several interesting diversions, however, from the American model. For one thing, the election of senators was national, not local, and the voters had a slate of candidates
from which to pick. The voters could also vote separately for
President and Vice-President, which meant that they could
vote for the presidential candidate from one party, and for
the vice-presidential candidate from the other party.

There were two major parties: the old-established Nacionalista Party, and the newly formed Liberals. Until the
end of the war, the Philippine Commonwealth had been a
virtual one-party country. The new young veterans wanted
something fresh, a party that spoke for *them*. Between the
two there was an almost total absence of ideological difference. Or there were *shades* of difference, illustrating the
Philippine genius for managing never to get anything quite
right: the Liberals did not become the party of the liberals,

any more than the Nacionalistas became the party of the nationalists. The Nacionalistas represented an old tolerant order, the Liberals a new impatient one.

The Philippine Republic, first of the new nations of the post-war world, was duly born on American Independence Day, 1946, in a pain too numbing for imagination to assess, in a loneliness to challenge the limits of compassion. True, the nations of Europe were a series of vast ruins just as the Philippines was, but they had each other's cultures to sustain them, and in a way they kept each other company. Berlin, contemplating its ruins, could, in a way, take comfort from Warsaw, which could measure itself against Dresden. Milan was a shambles, and so was London. But they were *there,* part of one European community, and starving and suffering equally. Manila was all alone in the world. It had nothing to judge by, no yardstick with which to measure the full scale of the disaster except itself. The nearest bombed city in the Allied world was Rangoon, in Burma, thousands of miles away. In the context of Allied victory, the destruction of Tokyo did not count.

The new nation, however, was rich in some ways. It was rich in guns. Throughout the war boatload after boatload of guns of all kinds had been dumped in the Philippines to aid the guerrillas against the Japanese, and by the end of the war it was estimated that in the islands there were five guns to every adult male of the population. And it was difficult after three years of killing Japanese and stealing from them as a patriotic duty to ask the Filipinos to stop killing and stealing. It was the only way that millions knew how to survive.

As in all devastated countries, there were quick fortunes to be made. In addition to the guns, stockpiles of military equipment lay all over the island worth an estimated billion dollars, an Aladdin's Cave of hardware: jeeps, trucks, bulldozers, uniforms, rations, medical supplies. Quick-witted American and Filipino operators flourished in the ruins of Manila and became overnight millionaires.

The result was inevitable. The miraculous patriotism and moral fervor that had sustained the Filipinos during the war collapsed, as everybody scrabbled among the ruins to stay alive and, with luck, to make a fast buck. "Getting away with it" became a national philosophy, ranging from the top to the bottom, and the whole country lived by what was known as the *compadre* system. The *compadre* is, in effect, a kind of godfather, in the literal, not the Mafioso sense. The godfather's obligation to his own people was total. A person needing help came to his *compadre* not with a request, but considering he had a *right* to assistance. Anyone taking a responsible job, with the power to hire and fire, hired his *compadres,* and nepotism was rife. It is only fair to say that the practice never reached the Malacañang Palace itself. It is a saving miracle of democracy that the person who reaches up and achieves the absolute pinnacle of power tends to be an honest man. If he were not, he would have been found out on the way up. But the corruption in the Philippines certainly washed right up to the presidential gates, as Cabinet Ministers checked their guns and openly smoked their contraband cigarettes at Cabinet meetings.

Apart from all the economic nightmares facing the baby republic there was the emotional problem of collaboration with the Japanese, from puppet President José Laurel down to the little man in the street who could survive only by speculating or supplying the Japanese with goods. President Osmeña anticipated the problem from the moment he landed with General MacArthur, and made a speech of amazing moderation and magnitude for such an emotional moment. He pointed out that during the enemy occupation not everyone could take to the mountains, and that those Filipinos who remained at their jobs but were prompted to protect their people, or feared enemy reprisal, were not traitors. (This makes an illuminating comparison with bloodthirsty sentiments expressed in civilized capitals like Paris and Brussels, both recently liberated from the Germans and hellbent on settling the scores of occupation, and a few others as well. In France and Belgium, the problem of collaboration as against resistance remains a crisis of conscience to this day, and as recently as February 1973, the coffin of Marshal Pétain was stolen by right-wing French sympathizers.) The Filipinos decently buried the whole issue by granting an amnesty in January 1948. José Laurel was not only rehabilitated, but actually ran for President again in 1949, for the Nacionalistas.

By the time independence came, the Philippines had a new President. National elections were set for April 1946. President Osmeña represented the Nacionalistas, who had led the union since 1907. The Liberals' candidate was one of the nation's heroes, Manuel Roxas. Roxas, an *ilustrado,* born in 1892, had been an active politician before the war.

During the first Philippine campaign he served at Bataan,
Corregidor, and Mindanao. He was captured by the Japanese, and pretended to agree to collaborate with them, but
instead he masterminded guerrilla operations in Luzon from
his office in Manila. Roxas was one of the presidential party
of José Laurel which the Japanese were transporting back to
Japan, but he eluded his guard, escaped, and met up with
the Americans on April 15, 1945. MacArthur promoted him
to general immediately.

While Roxas stumped the archipelago in the American
fashion, Osmeña remained aloof from the campaign, and
sat at his desk in Malacañang, attending to the immediate
needs of the starving nation. Despite Roxas's popular appeal
and Osmeña's hauteur, the result was a close one, and
Osmeña was only narrowly defeated. Osmeña was the first
to congratulate his opponent and severely discouraged his
followers from expressing resentment. In a broadcast he
stated that Filipinos should abide by the decision of the electorate, and he urged them to cooperate with the new Chief
Executive. He wished good luck to the President-elect and
then retired from public life, to live quietly, tending his
garden, reading and praying at his home in Cebu. Five years
later, on July 4, 1950, Osmeña, this dedicated man, was ac-
claimed the greatest living Filipino statesman. He died in
1960, aged eighty-two.

Roxas was a withdrawn, serious man from the province
of Capiz, who smiled seldom. He was very Spanish in his
habits, using English with an appearance of reluctance. He

seemed to be more a man of science than a poet, not to be quickly affected by impulses of emotion or sentiment. Of all his problems, the greatest were poverty and inequity.

While new millionaires erupted into elegant residential districts like Forbes Park, money for welfare simply was not there. Slums like the historic, but noisome, Tondo district of Manila spread into neighboring areas. The countryside grew even poorer, the sharecroppers sinking ever more deeply into debt to the landowners. These peasants were at the end of their tether. Through succeeding régimes, both friendly and savage, their lot never changed. Spaniards, Americans, Japanese, and their own people left them as they were. They remained the serfs of the landowners, and they lived and worked to pay back the money they owed to the Chinese moneylenders. Amply, they filled the words of Thomas Hobbes, the seventeenth-century philosopher when he wrote, "No arts; no letters; no society, and which is worst of all, continual fear and danger of violent death; and the life of man, solitary, poor, nasty, brutish and short." He forgot one other adjective, "fecund." They poured more and more wretched infants into their wretched world, in such numbers that even serious reform promised to be overwhelmed.

Manila was well enough aware of the problem, but the obstacles were heartbreaking. The average wage for industrial workers was 8 pesos, or just over a dollar a day, and for agricultural workers 6 pesos, 50 centavos. The average national wage stood at a wretched $180 a year. (Lest such an income seem totally incomprehensible, it should be added that the clothing needs in such a hot country are minimal, the cost of food is little more than one percent of American costs, and the Filipino peasants meet many of their needs by barter.)

No one can ever assess whether Roxas, the nation's hero, would have been a forthright President, because he served only two years of his term. Dynamism and courage on the field of battle do not necessarily qualify a man for the highest office of the land.

In April 1948, he addressed officers and men of the 13th U.S. Air Force at Clark Field. The period was one of the tensest and most edgy of the Cold War. None of the world's nations, with the exception of the United States, had recovered from the battering of World War II. Malnutrition was world-wide. War-weary people lived in bombed-out cities, and the menace of Stalin's Russia loomed more frighteningly all the time. Only the month before, the Communists had seized democratic Czechoslovakia in a *coup d'état*. The nationalist Chinese of General Chiang Kai Shek seemed incapable, despite tremendous American assistance in money and weapons, of maintaining any sort of a coherent front against the expanding Communist armies of Mao Tse Tung. The diplomats, strategists, and ordinary people of the world wondered, trembling, where Communism would strike next.

In his speech, very courageous for the head of a State so close to China, President Roxas warned that if the Soviet Union dared to trample further on the freedom of democratic peoples, the Americans and the Filipinos would again unite to stop the aggressors. He had hardly stepped down from the rostrum when he collapsed and died later from a heart attack. Roxas, as a soldier and a statesman, had literally exhausted himself to death in the service of his country.

The decade of the forties, begun in comparative peace, and with high hopes for the coming of independence for the Philippines, passed through the tragic years of war with Japan, and ended with the nation prostrate, on a collision course with calamity and all-out civil war. And to cap it all, the President had followed Quezon into the grave. Both destiny and desperation now met and distilled themselves into a poison which seized on the enfeebled Philippines, and came close to breaking its spirit altogether. The poison was called the Huks.

Chapter 10

THE HUKS

"Huk" is a word redolent of savagery, as evocative as other
monosyllables that have inspired terror throughout history,
from the "Huns" and "Turks" to the "Thugs" of the Khyber
Pass. During the Japanese occupation of the Philippines,
one of the best-organized guerrilla forces, operating from
north of Manila all the way to Baguio, was the Hukbong
Mapagpagpalayang Bayan, shortened locally to the Hukbalahap, and for headline purposes to the Huks. The original
title is Tagalog for People's Liberation Army, and students
of post-war political history have learned, usually rightly,
that when the word "people" is introduced, it means that
the Communists have taken over, and it is time for all good
democrats to run for cover.

The Huk period of domination in the Philippines extended for eight years, from 1946 until they were finally

broken in 1954, necessitating a war longer than the French fought for Indo-China in the same period, and as long as the United States subsequently waged against North Viet Nam. The breeding ground of the Huks was the impoverished farmland, the fishponds, and marshes where the share-croppers lived in their perpetual bondage. The Hukbalahap itself was not strictly or exclusively Communist. But the area had been heavily indoctrinated by the Communists, not least by American Communists who had sent missionaries of revolt into the *barrios* in the 1920s. The Huks operated faith-fully on the twin Communist principles of carrot and stick, of reward and murder. As reward for the peasants they took over *cacique* lands and redistributed them to the peasants themselves. Not surprisingly, they were widely held to be heroes and Robin Hoods. They also rounded up bandits who stole *carabaos,* and executed them in the village square.

As a warning, anyone who stood in their way was killed, whether the opposition was expressed physically or in terms of dialectic. The victims would most probably be the local mayors, lawyers, police chiefs. These they gathered under the blanket term "collaborators." During the war it was esti-mated that the Huks killed four times as many "collabora-tors" as they killed Japanese. And they killed many Japanese.

At the end of the war, the Huks were given what they bitterly considered to be a raw deal. Partly because of their dubious politics, partly because they had formed, in effect, a government of their own during the war, they were ex-cluded from the wartime pay, decorations, and booty dis-tributed among the other guerrillas. This exclusion brought their anti-social anger to revolutionary level. To make their grievances worse, President Roxas's executive refused to seat seven congressmen who had been elected with Huk backing, among them the leader of the Hukbalahap himself, Luis Taruc. Taruc was a small, handsome, unsmiling, humorless man, born an *ilustrado,* educated as a Catholic, an intellectual Communist, who, as the world knows, tends to be far more dangerous than the working-class Communist. To the intellectual Communist there is no sound so melodious as the thud of his own society biting the dust.

The areas of Luzon which the Huks had taken over they now proceeded to widen, which meant a head-on clash with the forces of law and order. The Huk victories were consistent and seemingly irreversible. Today, such a story is an old one, but then it was new, and terrifying to the ordinary citizen. The Philippine Army and the constabulary controlled the towns, and the rebels controlled the countryside. The government forces controlled the day, and locked themselves behind barbed wire by night, leaving the vital hours of darkness to the Huks.

Worse, the Philippine Army and police were demoralized by poor and intermittent pay. Corruption was widespread. They sometimes ill-treated and robbed the villagers, taking away their chickens and rice without payment, which the Huks never did. One of the nastiest practices was for the absentee landlords to send their bailiffs along on army sweeps to collect debts and back rents. As the peasants had had to pay dues to the Huks, and had no opportunity of keeping ahead of their obligations, they often had to give up more than half of their harvests. (Cynics may say the same is true of the American taxpayer, but the subsistence level of the Philippine rural worker's life ceases to give relevance to the joke.) For the army the countryside was hostile, dangerous, a place of invisible terror. Like army units in similar situations, before and since, they frequently panicked, wiping out villages and their entire populations, if they thought they had been harboring the Huks. In this period, for the Philippines, nothing ever seemed to go right.

It is as well for the Philippine people and the frail democracy they were trying so hard and conscientiously to nurture, against all odds, that they were not granted the gift of foresight. Otherwise they would have admitted defeat on the spot. Contemporary students will find the story so irresistibly parallel to the situation in Viet Nam that they would be excused for predicting that the Philippine government and its democracy were doomed. They would argue, pointing to Viet Nam, that no government, especially corrupt government, can win a war against a Communist-oriented peasant movement seeking to redress legitimate grievances.

The two styles of government were diametrically different. Faced with an incompetent bureaucracy, the Huks simply took over the land and redistributed it. The ordinary Filipino in the street, faced with the same bureaucracy, waved a banknote at it, and moved to the top of the line. There was no doubt which method made the greater appeal to the peasant.

Ironically, the biggest financial backer of the Huks was the United States government. Clark Field and other U.S.

Army installations were so deep in Huk territory that the American army had to use armed convoys to transfer men and supplies. The army employed 6,500 Filipinos for various tasks, and all of them paid their taxes to the Huks. Off-base, U.S. troops would descend on the sleazy soldier-city of Angeles, a three-mile strip of honky-tonks, brothels, and bars. Every person in Angeles—the taxi-drivers, prostitutes, bartenders, jitney drivers—paid the Huks a fixed proportion of their tips. The U.S. Army spent at this period an average of 75,000 dollars a day in Angeles, and the Huk coffers were enriched by an estimated half million dollars.

After the death of Manuel Roxas, the presidency passed to his Vice-President Elpidio Quirino, who was then fifty-eight years old. Although the presidency was supposed to run for four years, as in the United States, the Philippines had had five presidents in less than four years (Quezon, Laurel, Osmeña, Roxas, Quirino), and Quirino was the second Vice-President in that time to rise to the presidency.

Quirino was rich, aristocratic, a small, chubby man, with a deceptively placid face. He hid a keen mind, a quick wit, and a considerable idealism behind an air of worldliness and cynicism. During the war he had endured a spell in Fort Santiago Prison for aiding the guerrillas, and an experience in that most horrible of dungeons can quench the fighting spirit of the strongest. Like every other Filipino he had suffered terrible tragedy during the war. His wife and two children had been shot dead by the Japanese during the liberation of Manila, and he had resolved to spend the rest of his life a widower.

Quirino tried first to appease the Huks, a far from un-reasonable measure. He realized that the Americans, by denying the Huks their wartime pay, were condemning them to return to their old peonage. Quirino amnestied the Huks and invited Luis Taruc to Malacañang almost as though he were a visiting head of State. Taruc became a guest of the palace, and was informed that the President had created a Presidential Action Committee to promote the welfare of the rural masses.

Taruc refrained from mentioning that Huk plans for a takeover were too advanced to be stopped. August 15, 1949 had been named as the deadline for the Huks to surrender under the amnesty, but only a handful had given up their arms. When Taruc was sought for an explanation he did not reply, because he was not there. He had disappeared, van-ished into the hills, and from his secret hideout he issued a manifesto stating that the only real friend and ally of the Philippines was the Soviet Union.

With a feeling of dread, the Philippine government pre-pared for a new war. Roadblocks were set up in the outskirts of the capital. The brutal climax came in April 1949, when Mrs. Aurora Quezon, widow of the Commonwealth Presi-dent, was ambushed and shot dead while traveling to the province of Tayabas. With her died her daughter, her son-in-law, and six officials. She had been on her way to officiate at the province's ceremony, in which its name was to be changed to Quezon. The murder was, in fact, an accident. The Huks thought they were ambushing Quirino. The pub-lic was sickened, and in a climate of fear and hate, the nation prepared for—of all things—a general election.

The 1949 election is remembered in the Philippines as "the dirty election." Quirino, representing the Liberals, ran against José Laurel standing for the Nacionalistas. Both sides were guilty of terrorism. Goon squads guarded the voting booths and kept people cowering in their homes by firing guns in the streets. Several hundred people were killed. The Huks backed the Nacionalistas. Quirino won, but only narrowly, and many of Laurel's supporters took to the hills. Among the candidates elected to the Senate for the first time in this election were two future Presidents of the Philippines, Diosdado Macapagal, and Ferdinand Marcos, both of the Liberal Party.

After the election, the civil war began. Several of Taruc's chief lieutenants went to Moscow where they were kindly received. The Huks carried out systematic attacks on villages and towns, until large areas of Central Luzon became almost undisputed Huk territory. They throve in Pampanga, Tarlac, Pangasinan, Cavite, Laguna, and around Mount Arayat. They would occupy a *barrio,* arrest the mayor and the town lieutenant, and shoot them in the principal plaza, ordering the villagers to leave the bodies untouched.

Manila itself ceased to be safe. An unofficial curfew was declared, and troops with fixed bayonets patrolled residential districts. In Malacañang Palace, a secret tunnel built by the Spaniards two hundred years before was unsealed to enable the President to make a quick getaway if the palace was stormed.

Neither the constabulary nor the army could find the key to stop the Huks. The army was more disciplined than the

police, but was demonstrating, like the French in Indo-
China, that a fine resistance or guerrilla record in wartime
does not necessarily provide suitable training for conventional warfare. One of the problems, as in all guerrilla wars,
was that, on entering a *barrio,* they could not tell who was
a Huk and who was not, and many innocent villagers suffered punishment, beatings, and even death.

The year 1950 marked the nadir in the fortunes of the
Philippines since the war. As if civil war were not enough,
corruption was rife in the capital, reaching monumental pro-
portions in politics, business, the army, and the bureaucracy.
A few Filipinos might take comfort from Gibbon's definition of corruption as "the most infallible symptom of constitutional liberty," but it was no way to run a country. To be
fair, it should be said that President Quirino's eyes were on
wider horizons. He was no innovator of policies. He was an
administrator, and his ideas were the ideas of Roxas. He was
a Weygand to Roxas's Foch, and the temperament of a
chief of staff is not necessarily that of a commander in chief.
Quirino's real interest was in foreign affairs. Insofar as he
was doing what he set out to do, Quirino was notably successful, and as a result, the Philippines in this period had two
completely unrelated images.

To the Filipinos themselves, the country appeared to be
one vast den of corruption, a paradise for any kind of racket-
eer and crooked business operator. To the outside world, the
Philippines was admired as a new country that was seriously
trying to make constitutional democracy work against all the
hazards of Communist insurrection and infiltration. It was

a model of moderation and reason in world affairs, and an example, in its sober foreign policy, to new nations everywhere. And both images were correct. If Quirino is to go down in history as a President who condoned monumental corruption at home, he is also to be respected for the enviable place that the Philippines assumed in world affairs.

In the course of 1950, in a despairing move, President Quirino summoned to Malacañang, for advice, a fifty-two year-old United States Air Force colonel, Edward L. Lansdale. Lansdale is one of the most interesting, and in many ways the most mysterious man in modern American military history, a man more suited to English or French military eccentricity than to the more Germanified American military traditions. He was a loner above all. He saw that there was more to any given military situation than merely winning battles, or even wars. His thinking was in the direct tradition of Lawrence of Arabia, or Colonel Godard's French Condor groups in Indo-China.

Lansdale did not look the part of cloak-and-dagger man. With his straight carriage and clipped mustache he looked like the typical clean-limbed pre-war West Pointer, or, more disturbingly, like the American officer-caricature favored in Japanese propaganda photographs, emerging haggard-looking from Bataan or Corregidor, with his hands in the air, wearing a World War I tin helmet.

Although a flyer, Lansdale was, in some ways, an infantryman *manqué*. He made a specialized study of infantry tactics, especially scouting, patroling and other forms of small-unit operation. He was deeply impressed by the intelligence and individualism of British operations in Malaya, which proved that even the most ideologically motivated guerrillas can be defeated both in military action and psychological argument. He was aware that the essential in guerrilla warfare is not to kill rebels, not, in the terminology of a later war, to make a head count. The essential is to find a viable alternative to Communist philosophy, and at the same time make the people in the villages feel secure from attack by either side. To achieve the latter objective, the forces of law must produce some leader that the people can turn to, to see that justice is done, someone who would listen to their appeals.

The details of Lansdale's talks with the President are not on record. He most certainly pressed home his philosophical points of view, but the question remained, what military leader existed in the Philippines who could rally a demoralized people to fight back against the Huks, and restore the wartime emotions of patriotic fervor. Such a man would have to have exceptional qualities, because even Manuel Roxas had not been able to succeed in the task. Quirino, bland, intellectual, as smooth as an egg, was most emphatically not the man the nation could look to for deliverance. What the Philippines needed, in short, was a knight in shining armor carrying a sword aloft, a man of magic and charisma. It so happened that Edward Lansdale knew just such a man, his own protégé, one Ramon Magsaysay, the senator from Zambales.

Chapter 11

"THE GUY"

WHAT AN INCREDIBLE people the Filipinos are! Where so many countries, bigger, and with more continuous civilizations, can produce no more than one major figure, or two, or perhaps three, to illuminate their history books, the Philippines spews them out, larger than life, swaggering through the pages of the nation's history, often coming to sticky ends, often motivated by questionable ideals, but making history all the more exciting to outsiders because their stories are largely unread and can consequently be studied with new excitement, like reading a splendid book for the first time.

On the urging of Lansdale, President Quirino appointed Ramon Magsaysay to his Cabinet as Secretary of Defense. Magsaysay had just turned forty. He was little known to the country generally, although he was a well-known figure in Zambales, a mountainous province, which sticks out of the map of Luzon like a boxer's left ear. Zambales is rugged country, producing a hardy, thrifty people not unlike the highlanders of Scotland. It was also a Huk stronghold.

Because he shone so brilliantly and so briefly over the Asian scene, there has been a good deal of legend added to the facts of Magsaysay's life. One of the most persistent is that he came from a poor family, and was thus the first man who was not an *ilustrado* to reach the summits of Philippine public life. The Magsaysays were not rich, but they were not peasants. Magsaysay's father was a schoolteacher, and well connected, and Ramon, or "Monching" as his friends called him, graduated from high school and then took up engineering at the University of the Philippines. He was a fanatical enthusiast of anything mechanical, and he could take derelict cars and make them race. He began his career as a bus mechanic with a firm of passenger buses, married the boss's daughter, and succeeded in making a sagging business show a profit.

Magsaysay was a tough-looking fellow with a huge grin. He stood 5 feet 11 inches, very tall for a Filipino. He laughed readily, and loved funny stories, not least his own. His rugged appearance was deceptive because, as a youth, he had been turned down by the U.S. Army for medical reasons. He was thirty-four years old when the Japanese attacked Pearl Harbor, and enlisted in the 31st U.S. Infantry Motor Pool, tinkering with the engines. After the fall of Bataan, in which he did not take part, he escaped from the Japanese, and made his way home to organize resistance in Zambales. In time he was commanding ten thousand men, and, in 1945, he and his troops, after a bitter battle, captured the vitally important Zambales airstrip for the Americans to land on. He was appointed military governor of the province, and promoted to the rank of major by General MacArthur.

His success continued in the political world. He was elected congressman for the Liberal Party, and served on the Armed Forces Committee of the House. Unlike most Philippine congressmen, who tended to affect conservative American dress, he wore the *barong tagalog,* the lovely hand woven shirt made of pine fiber, traditional to the Philippines. No one today ever thinks of Magsaysay in anything but the *barong tagalog.* It is as inescapable a part of his historical image as Churchill's cigar. Subsequent Presidents, Macapagal and Marcos, have affected the *barong tagalog,* but it is always associated, not only in the Philippine mind, but in that of the rest of the world, with Magsaysay.

Magsaysay accepted responsibility for his new post with the kind of energy Malays usually leave to the Chinese. Filipinos adore catchy slogans, and Magsaysay introduced two which immediately caught the imagination, "Land for the landless," and "Those who have less in life should have more in law." (It was clear from the start that Magsaysay, unlike most Philippine politicians, was not a lawyer!)

On his first day in office he fired several high-ranking army officers. Next day he sent into the field officers who had implanted themselves in comfortable offices. His orders were short, pungent, and frequently delivered in person. He remolded the army, recasting the regular force around battalion combat teams of about 1,200 men each. Those units which had given a poor performance were recalled for re-training. Those who had fought well were made aware that the Secretary of Defense himself knew it, and was proud of them.

What Magsaysay was doing in the Philippines was what General de Lattre de Tassigny was doing for the equally demoralized French Army in Indo-China at the same time, turning morale upside down, making the soldiers believe in themselves, and making the enemy quake.

Magsaysay personally led his men into the various Huk territories, many of which he knew well from boyhood, eating and sleeping with the soldiers under the stars. He strode or jeeped through the *barrios,* and listened to all the villagers' complaints. He personally ordered, and made sure, that the soldiers and police behaved correctly to the villagers, paying for everything they took. Wherever he discovered local bitterness, he sought the origins, and attacked them. To convince the sharecropping families that they would get a better deal than their fathers, grandfathers, and greatgrandfathers, he assigned officers with law degrees to represent them against the landowners. Those who held back their help for fear of Huk reprisals, he promised virgin lands in Mindanao with tools and easy loans. He discovered that most of the soldiers were of peasant stock, ordered about hither and thither by a disproportionately large number of officers. Magsaysay introduced a policy of promotion to both commissioned and non-commissioned ranks on merit, and not on the compadre system.

It was a spectacular show, dear to the Philippine heart,

and the people loved it, and christened Magsaysay "the Guy." Intelligence on Huk movements poured in. Inevitably, he was obliged to meet accusations of "brutality" from lawyers living safely in Manila. His opponents charged that he was as ruthless as the Huks themselves, that he resorted to ambush, chicanery, lies, and torture, and fought terrorism with counter-terrorism. To all this he replied with frankness, point by point, in forthright words which reveal fully the temperament of the man:

> I had to fight fire with fire. No fighting is pretty and guerrilla warfare is probably the worst. Sure, we ambushed 'em, whenever we had the chance. They were trying to ambush us, weren't they? Sure we deceived them, to the best of our ability. Torture? No, not to my knowledge, and certainly not with my consent. I did not want to get my information that way. But this much I can say. No man who honestly surrendered in the belief that he would receive fair treatment had any reason to complain. We had hundreds of them and they were treated from the beginning as prisoners of war. Later we tried to do something good with them. But we never did lure any innocent man into a surrender trap by kind words and then cut his head off. That was not our way. I couldn't control every little squad in the field, and there may have been cases of what . . . call "excesses." They did not have my sanction. In fact, to cut down the chance of private revenge, I tried to make it a practice to put men into action in provinces or *barrios* where they could not have had any family connections. I tried to tell them that this was not the time to settle private grudges. It was a time to fight for our country.

All at once the Huks found that the regular forces were moving faster than they were, and that the soldiers also knew where the Huks were heading for. Magsaysay's men, as they now called themselves, routed them out of their strongholds in the Sierra Madre Mountains and killed them there, often in bloody encounters. His men splashed through the swamps and the fishponds of Pampanga and left Huks dead among the oysters, clams, and milk-fish.

One of the Huks' trumps lay in the high quality of their Intelligence which operated from within Manila itself, flashing information to all Huk areas about military movements. Magsaysay saw that if the Intelligence supply could be choked off the whole Huk movement would disintegrate. How he broke the Huks in Manila is one of the most extraordinary episodes of his career. He had been invited to "discussions" with some Huk leaders in the notorious Tondo area of Manila. It was stipulated that he should come alone, and unarmed, late at night. He accepted the challenge even though he knew he was probably signing his own death warrant. But his arrogance caught the Huks off guard. They had not dreamed that he would take them up on their offer, and Magsaysay found only one startled Huk, who agreed to switch sides when offered amnesty and a reward. Magsaysay learned that messages were transmitted from one Huk group to another by means of a woman who delivered vegetables. The woman was observed and followed. Each house at which she called was noted.

Magsaysay struck, achieving a success such as he had never dreamed of. The twenty-two houses at which she called were the headquarters of every Huk leader in the capital. One hundred and five conspirators were arrested. Forty-two thousand pesos in cash, the operating finances of the

Manila Communist Party, were seized with a huge cache of arms, including submachine guns, revolvers, hand grenades, and rifles.

But of even greater importance was the documentation. Magsaysay's men loaded five truckloads of papers which, when sorted out, proved to be the archives of the entire Red organization, a complete roster of all the party members in the country, their friends, sympathizers, and financiers, many of whom were prominent Chinese business men. Regional commanders and political supervisors were listed, and so were detailed military plans for the military take-over of the country, including the takeover of Manila for which the deadline of December 10, 1950 had been set.

Organized Huk resistance was over, even though the struggle continued for several years. But above all, the Philippine people had the knight in shining armor for whom they had sighed so long.

Older, and more cynical political observers could see that much of Magsaysay's magic was a mere shot in the arm, and that Magsaysay's brand of speed might induce unpleasant withdrawal symptoms. But under its impetus the Huk movement had collapsed. Fear disappeared from Manila, and self-confidence began to assert itself in the *barrios*. The Philippine people began to believe in themselves again.

Chapter 12

AND IN THE END, IT WAS ONLY
A FLASH IN THE SKY

OF COURSE, THE cynics were right. In dealing with the Philippines it is invariably wise to err on the side of the excessively pessimistic. The year 1950 had been the year in which the Communist offensive had been broken on three fronts by three leaders of genius. Magsaysay had licked the Huks. General MacArthur turned a summer disaster into a winter of triumph and annihilated the North Koreans by his action at Inchon. In Indo-China, General de Lattre de Tassigny, a French officer of aristocratic birth yet whose temperament was similar in so many ways to that of the ex-garage mechanic from Zambales, revived a beaten French Army and thrashed the Viet Minh of General Giap at Nam Dinh.

But these holes blasted in the international Communist lines soon filled in again. Reasons of politics compelled the United Nations forces to yield up the North Korea it had

133

liberated right up to the Yalu River. De Lattre died at a
moment when he could be least spared, and the French
sagged until they sank in the apocalyptic defeat at Dien Bien
Phu in 1954. In the Philippines the cracking of the Huk
forces was followed by a long and frustrating campaign of
pacification during which the Huks retreated to the mountains. It was two years before Luis Taruc, the Huk chief,
surrendered and entered into the darkness of prison to contemplate his own soul for the next twelve years, handing
over the ideological leadership of the Huks to his nephew,
Pedro Taruc.

Politics now takes over the Philippine scene. President
Quirino directed Magsaysay to work on clearing the virgin
lands in Mindanao and Palawan. Resettlement colonies were
opened for any Huks who cared to surrender, and each family was given a farm and land of between fifteen and
twenty-five acres with food and loans. Each of the new
colonies was interlaced with army veterans to prevent a
closing of the ideological ranks among the ex-Communists.

Magsaysay's chief task however was to put the army to
work to avoid a repetition of the "dirty election" of 1949.
Mid-term elections were due in 1951, and the troops patrolled the polling booths to make sure there was no intimi-
dation. The result was an overwhelming defeat for Quirino's
Liberal Party. All nine Liberal senators up for re-election
were defeated by the Nacionalistas. Quirino's own brother
ran bottom of the poll. Ex-President José Laurel, who
seemed to be made of India rubber, bounced back again, this
time into the Senate.

Although Magsaysay's party, and his President, were thoroughly discredited throughout the country, Magsaysay's own light shone brighter than ever. The demand of "Magsaysay for President" was overwhelming, as was the urge to cross party lines, and join the Nacionalistas. José Laurel, so narrowly defeated for president in 1949, strongly backed Magsaysay for 1953.

Relations between Quirino and Magsaysay, warm until now, deteriorated seriously. Quirino believed, with some reason, that Magsaysay was grabbing the credit for the policies which he, Quirino, had initiated. Magsaysay was resentful of the web of intrigue and nepotism with which he believed Quirino was surrounded.

Party-switching is an unusual move in any democratic country, and, being largely an act of desperation, is generally the prelude to political eclipse. Churchill, being Churchill, was able to do it twice, from Tory to Liberal and then back to Tory. In the United States, Wayne Morse of Oregon switched from Republican to Independent to Democrat in the 1950s, Mayor John Lindsay of New York switched from Republican to Democrat in 1972, and former Governor John Connally of Texas went the other way in 1973. But examples are rare.

The main precedent in the Philippines dated back to 1922, when Manuel Quezon denounced as autocratic the leadership of Sergio Osmeña and bolted from the Nacionalistas to form a party of his own. He concluded one of his famous bravura speeches with the words, "My loyalty to my party ends where my loyalty to my country begins." Thus beginning, as a leading Nacionalista said cynically, "the era of patriots." Whenever a politician fell out with his leadership, all he had to do was "quote Quezon and bolt."

Throughout 1952 and early 1953 rumors accumulated among the political quidnuncs of Manila that Magsaysay was plotting to switch in time for the election. It was the talk of the salons. In this case Quirino was rather in the position of a wife whose husband has been unfaithful to her, the "last to know." "I have every faith in the loyalty of R.M.," he told his highly dubious relatives.

It is probable that any cause would have been an excuse for a break, and it came in February 1953, on a question of further amnesty for the Huks. Magsaysay was against any such move, on the grounds that the Huks were on the run anyway. Quirino went over Magsaysay's head, ordered a cease-fire, and Magsaysay resigned. In the letter of resignation, Magsaysay widened the reasons for his disaffection. He said he had become disgusted with a government that was "full of crooks and grafters."

The election battle lines were established, almost inevitably: Quirino versus Magsaysay. In view of Quirino's unpopularity, the issue was not in question, and the most interesting aspect of the election is the curious part played in it by General Carlos P. Romulo.

Romulo was, and is, the Filipino best known to Americans for his remarkable oratory and fluent writing, and his urbane and witty representation of the Philippines both in the United Nations and in Washington. In the United Nations he had demonstrated by his articulateness and sophistication the importance of small nations when their arguments are well presented and without demagogy.

An *ilustrado* from Tarlac, Romulo began as a newspaperman and a publisher of the Philippines *Herald,* and won the Pulitzer Prize in journalism in 1941, the first Filipino ever to receive this honor, for his political observations on the Southeast Asian political situation. He became a soldier shortly before the Japanese arrived, beginning as press officer on the staff of General MacArthur. He served on Bataan and at Corregidor, withdrew with MacArthur to Australia, and finished the war a general.

In a nation not noted for its energy, Romulo was a dynamo, and task succeeded task in bewildering succession: resident commissioner of the Philippines to America in 1944; head of the Philippine delegation to the United Nations Conference in 1945; later permanent delegate; later Ambassador to the U.S. A small man with a round, tanned face, he resembled not only physically, but also by his wit, brilliance, impudence, egotism, and calculated indiscretion, no one so much as the Canadian publisher-statesman-soldier, Lord Beaverbrook. He was a veritable Philippine beaver.

In 1953, Romulo was the Philippine Ambassador in Washington and was not in sympathy with the administration in his own country. He was tired of the sneers he was having to take from the rather patronizing State Department about the corruption and maladministration at home. He also knew that Quirino was a weary man, in poor health. Romulo knew he had powerful support of his own in university and newspaper circles, and that several "Romulo for President" clubs had been formed. He returned to Manila and declared himself a candidate for the Liberal nomination in opposition to Quirino, but quickly decided that the con-

vention would be rigged, walked out, and formed a new
Democratic Party.

A new party always lacks the organization and the ma-
chinery of the established parties, and Romulo was soon
aware of the fact. He had not, until now, been a notable
admirer of Magsaysay. His view was that Magsaysay lacked
the education and experience to hold the office of President
of the Philippines. But there was no mistaking the trend in
the country, and the enthusiasm that "the Guy" engendered
everywhere. All sorts of American-style movements were
formed: Philippine Women for Magsaysay, Students for
Magsaysay, and so on. It is one of the facts of democracy that
the ultimate crown is denied the person best fitted for it.
Romulo was the best-equipped and most able man for the
job of President, but this was not the year for his kind of
wisdom. Realizing that, Romulo threw his party to Magsaysay, became Magsaysay's campaign manager, and Magsaysay won by the largest popular vote in Philippine history.

Edward Lansdale had done his job, and now that his man
had achieved the presidency, it was time for him to move
on, to seek other wars and meet other challenges. He flew to
Viet Nam just as the French were leaving as the result of
the disastrous defeat of the French Army by the North Vietnamese at Dien Bien Phu. Already the vacuum being left by
the French in Viet Nam was requiring another power to fill
it, and the only power that could do it was the United States.
No one foresaw the decades of misery that would follow.
Henry Cabot Lodge, the American emissary in Saigon,

summoned Lansdale and asked him to do for Viet Nam what he had done for the Philippines: discover some political figure of stature around whom the South Vietnamese could unite.

Lansdale studied the political and military situation and decided that his man was Ngo Dinh Diem. Diem, a Catholic, and a strong nationalist of autocratic instinct, was soon tangling with most of the other military and religious factions in the country. To an extent it could be said that he repeated the Magsaysay performance, by becoming the country's strong man. Lansdale, now a general, withdrew in 1957, and collapse soon followed in Viet Nam. Diem's unorthodox procedures and his strong anti-Buddhist beliefs worried the United States. An anti-Diem campaign grew in momentum and he was, in due course, assassinated. In the simplistic labeling of history, Diem is a "baddie," a dictator who laughed when Buddhists immolated themselves in protest at his policies. A more realistic judgment was offered by Wilfred Burchett, the authoritative Australian correspondent who covers wars from the Communist side. He said that the death of Diem was hailed with delight by the Viet Cong, who, from then on remained convinced that nothing could stop them.

Magsaysay's political victory generated an excitement throughout the Philippines not dissimilar to that in the United States nine years later at the election of John F. Kennedy. There was a feeling that something new and revolutionary had happened to the country, that a new element of glamor enfolded it. To dramatize the difference in styles: the new President, on his first day in office, canceled the inaugural ball and held a public reception instead, the people crowding over the lawns of Malacañang Palace to see the new Sun King with their own eyes.

And so Quirino, the last of the *ilustrados,* left the public scene. He was too much of an aristocrat to show the bitterness he undoubtedly felt. He had much to offer by way of consolation. He knew his record would be vindicated in time, as indeed it was. Quirino's departure marked the end of the rule of the Philippines by gentlemen, *ilustrados* who spoke in Tagalog to their servants, in English to the press, and in Spanish to their family and to God.

A handful of Liberals had survived the cataclysm of the election. One was Diosdado Macapagal and the other Ferdinand Marcos. It was clear that if the Liberal Party was ever to recover, it must be through one or the other of these men. But not both; their personalities were such that only one of the two could succeed as the leader of the party. Marcos's career had been enriched by a new, stunning, and very rich wife, Imelda Romualdez, a daughter of one of the Philippines's wealthiest sugar families. Imelda was also a cousin to the Speaker of the House, and a former beauty queen. Marcos, knowing that Macapagal was the biggest obstacle to his ambitions, made it quite plain in the political salons that the palace of Malacañang belonged to him, Marcos, and no one else, when Magsaysay's two terms expired eight years hence, in 1961.

Magsaysay listened well to the elder statesmen of the na-

tion, men who had no more political axes to grind. He succeeded in opening the window of Philippine politics to a
certain extent. He sought to see through temporary difficulties to the deeper problems of the Philippine nation. He
opened Malacañang to all who wanted to bring their trou-
bles to him, established a Complaints and Action Commission—a kind of Ombudsman group—to deal with complaints from private citizens, and heard sixty thousand complaints in one year, more than a thousand a week. He formed
a Court of Agrarian Relations to speed action on behalf of
the sharecroppers. He started action for the drilling of wells
to provide drinking water in the *barrios*. He took steps toward self-government in the *barrios* by having the villagers
elect their own councils to replace officials appointed on the
compadre system by municipal mayors.

He formed the National Resettlement and Rehabilitation
Administration, offering a migrant family a freehold of
1,000 pesos (then 500 dollars), and new tenancy laws guar-
anteeing a fairer share of the crop for the grower.

So completely did Magsaysay personify and symbolize his
people that the Liberal Party conceded defeat in advance
for the 1957 elections. It announced it would not put up a
presidential candidate but would concentrate on Congress
and on local, provincial, and municipal government.

The Philippines, which had been so cruelly ill used, and
had struggled so hard, deserved, by any judgment, the man
it had got. He had suffered when the country suffered. He
had saved the nation from Communism almost single-
handed, and raised it to the pinnacle of its international

prestige. But his hair had turned from black to gray in the effort. It seemed too good to last, and it was. It was as if such a man could not be bequeathed outright to a nation, but only loaned and then taken away.

At dawn on March 17, 1957, "Pinatubo," the plane of President Magsaysay, bound for Manila and critically over-loaded, crashed into Mount Manungal on the island of Cebu. Magsaysay was killed, and so was the entire comple-ment of the plane save one, the journalist, Nestor Mata. The man of action had died, probably as he wanted, and even as he did so some political observers felt that his reputation was saved by his death, that the impetus of his administra-tion had run its course and was about to run down. They argued that Magsaysay's reforms were little more than plas-ter, and the cracks were already showing through. A Con-gress dominated by landlords had failed to provide the neces-sary funds to make the reforms work. Relatively few of the hundreds of thousands of sharecroppers had been moved to the new colonies, and for everyone that was resettled another took his place. Where glimmers of improvement appeared they were rapidly extinguished by the new mouths to feed, as the population rose by a debilitating three percent a year, one of the highest in the world.

But they always say that of heroes—that they died at the right time. They said it about de Lattre de Tassigny in Indo-China. It was no consolation. Magsaysay was only forty-nine years old when he died.

The *New York Times* wrote: "The tragic death of Presi-dent Ramon Magsaysay has taken from the Philippines a great leader. His greatness lay in part in the very fact that he was so much of the Filipino people. He was no stranger to the most intimately human problems in the lives of the simplest of the folk he led. He was in and of his country as the truly great so often are. . . . Our friends in the Philippines will be right if they enshrine the memory of Magsaysay in the same glorious panel that has the names of Rizal and Bonifacio . . ."

One Filipino newspaper called Magsaysay's death "the blackest day in our history." Fantastic scenes were witnessed when the grounds of Malacañang Palace were opened for people to see the dead President lying in state. Hundreds of thousands lined up to pay their respects. They wept. Many fainted; some screamed with grief. He was more than a mere President. They had shaken his hand when he toured the *barrios* in his jeep. They had seen him and touched him. He had made them feel personally that they were important, a living part of the Philippine heritage.

Chapter 13

THE ERA OF FRAGILE POLITICS

THE NEW PRESIDENT—the former Vice-President—Carlos P. Garcia,* was at sixty older than the general run of Philippine politicians, a small, dark-skinned, curly-haired man, almost Moorish in appearance, a war hero who led guerrillas in his native Bohol against one of the densest concentrations of Japanese troops in the islands. The Japanese had offered a large reward for information leading to his capture, but no one could ever catch him. He was a rhetorician and a poet in the Visayan language. He loved long words, preferring "penumbra" to "shadow," "introspection" to "thought," "routinary" to "routine."

His habits and tastes were earthy. He did not even own

* Note the "P" in Carlos P. Garcia, and the "P" in Carlos P. Romulo. Filipinos who had once taken pride in the Spanish forms of nomenclature had now widely adopted the exclusively American style of the middle initial.

the right clothes in which to be sworn in as President. He enjoyed spending nights sitting around a table playing poker with the boys. Political observers, hoping for the best, compared his personality to that of former President Truman, and prayed fervently that Garcia, like Truman, would rise to fit the office he had inherited.

His prepared speeches were dreadful. He edited his speech writers, and made the result worse, but when he threw his notes away and spoke extempore he could reduce an audience to quite the wrong kind of tears. He was well known for his personal vanity, and refused to wear glasses although he needed them, and often offended friends by walking past them, unable to see them through the "penumbra" of his own vision. But he had the reputation of a winner. He had served two terms as congressman and three as a senator. It would have been difficult for any man to follow in the path of Magsaysay. Of Garcia it can be said that it seemed likely he would find it more difficult than most.

Garcia rose to the presidency in 1957. From then until the fateful year of 1972, when President Marcos declared martial law in the Philippines and suspended the democratic process, the story of the Philippines is the story of democratic politics, fascinating to the participants and to politically minded Filipinos, but somewhat less so to the uncommitted outside observer, so the reader will take a breather here to study the political climate of the Philippines as it extended through the years.

By the time of the death of Magsaysay and the swearing-in

of Garcia, the Philippines had performed a remarkable feat.
The country had passed through a shattering crisis of leadership without violence, without economic collapse or even the
suspicion of a *coup d'état*. The military had not moved, nor
had the police, and there had been no secret caucuses among
politicians. Such was the political maturity of the Filipinos
and their respect for constitutional process. As Robert Aura
Smith, the *New York Times*'s Asian scholar, was to observe,
any attempt by a usurper to take over the country would not
merely have been resisted; it would have been hooted at.
Political sophistication could go no further.

Few peoples in the world took to politics with more gusto
than the Filipinos. With a few exceptions, the highest offices
of the land were usually reserved for the *ilustrados* and the
dynastic families, but for the rest it was a game almost anyone with some kind of education or other could play. A law
degree was a great advantage, although not to the extent it
was in the United States. For an ambitious young man, politics was an escape from the dead end of the *barrios,* the
way boxing was in the United States for poor blacks, and
pop groups for the kids of Liverpool.

Because to be in politics one needed an education, shop-
front universities proliferated in the cities, offering degrees
that were almost worthless to the outside world, turning out
semi-educated graduates who called themselves intellectuals
but could scarcely write the English language, masters of
the cliché, to whom no one could be "honest" if he could be
"on the up-and-up," or "friendly" if he could be "palsy-
walsy." Never mind; the previous degree hung framed on

their walls as proof of qualification for higher things. As many of these graduates went on to become teachers, and even to write text books and do translations from the Spanish, the woeful standard of English at certain levels became self-perpetuating. *Noli Me Tangere* and *El Filibusterismo* suffered badly in this manner until Léon Ma. Guerrero applied himself to the task.

Many observers declared, and some Filipinos agreed, that the level of democracy achieved in the Philippines was roughly on a par with that of the United States in the McKinley era; the same addiction to demagogery and violence, the same passion for free and unbelievably strident newspapers in the style of the early William Randolph Hearst. The McKinley era in the United States nevertheless produced some great Americans, and this brash era of the Philippines did not prevent the emergence of great figures either.

The newspapers had to be experienced to be believed. The Philippines *was* a lawless society, with muggings in the streets, robberies, gang wars, drug pushing, all the evils of American society, but if the newspapers were to be believed, no citizen was safe in his bed. Crime was splashed across the front pages in headlines that scarcely left any room for text.

But to turn from the front pages to the inside pages was to enter a different world, a world where the standard of editorial opinion and comment was first-rate by any standards. The political columnists, like J. V. Cruz, Nestor Mata (the survivor of the Magsaysay air crash), and Nick Joaquin, were as brilliant as any in the United States, and more stylish than most. Jo Guevara, as a humorous political jester, was not quite in the class of Art Buchwald, but then nobody is. Guevara was certainly one of the best in the world. The political cartoonists were the equal of all but perhaps Mauldin and Herblock in the United States.

If one compares the Philippine political scene of the 1960s with the American political scene of the McKinley period, one can also make a comparison with the Third and Fourth Republics of France, both of which intrigued, corrupted, and stabbed each other into a state of such moral emasculation that they had to be put out of their agonies firstly by Marshal Pétain in 1940, and then by General de Gaulle in 1958.

In the smart salons of the villas in Forbes Park, Manila, the back-stabbing, character assassination, scandal-mongering, and general bitchiness often seemed to be right out of Paris, and wealthy political wives held court in a way that reminded one almost dizzily of Madame de Pompadour, a feeling heightened by the fact that in Manila the reality is always at such odds with the illusion. The hostesses tend to have names like Baby (no matter what age), Tingting, Chona, Chito, and Cherrypie. They are both beautiful and ageless, and the Westerner is frequently stunned when a lovely young woman engages him in conversation and talks about her eight grandchildren. Like the men, they are small, polite, smiling, and their English is singsong, rather slow, appears to rise a full octave when they are excited or upset, until it reaches a pitch calculated to ruffle the fur on a cat's back. The slow pace often gives the wildly incorrect illusion that it is labored. It is not so. Philippine children speak English like that from birth.

And behind the initial, rather childlike impression, the political ladies have wills of steel. Filipino politicians, male and female, are master polemicists, debaters, and conversationalists.

The author was present at a dinner party given for a monsignor from Rome and some of his aides. The monsignor spoke little English and no Spanish, so a rather pompous young Canadian Jesuit carried most of the conversation on his behalf. The subject of conversation was the great religious debate of the time, the degree of the culpability of Pope Pius XII in the death of six million Jews in Hitler's gas chambers.

The young priest was being submitted to murderous though always polite attack by his hosts, and he argued back, ably, not ducking any questions or taking any easy way out. "You must understand," he said, "the conditions of the priesthood in occupied Europe, and the tragic consequences if the Pope *did* decide to make a confrontation with Hitler on the subject. There is a letter in the Vatican archives from the priests of Rotterdam *begging* the Pope not to speak on the subject."

The hostess spoke up innocently, her Oriental eyes wide with interest. "So, Fahzzair (as she pronounced Father)," she said. "It was for the priests of Rotterdam that His Holiness decided not to say anything about the death of six million Jews." Zonk!

Physical beauty is important in Philippine politics, and it carries with it the backbiting that follows beauty everywhere. If some young society lady has a rather more Oriental cast of face than the general Malay faces around her, some hostess is going to wonder innocently whether there were any Japanese troops stationed near the home of her mother during the war. Such innuendoes are particularly popular when leveled against beauty queens, because beauty queens are considered great assets as wives of politicians (Mrs. Marcos and Mrs. Macapagal were both former beauty queens).

The next requirement is oratory. Filipinos, conditioned from birth to the splendors of the Church, enjoy a good show. They want to be entertained. Politicians are expected to entertain them, and university prizes in oratory are highly regarded. No *curriculum vitae* is ever complete without such laudatory comments as "he excelled in public speaking and debating, and was elected president of the Debating Society in high school." High school and university debates are recalled in later years with the fondness which sports fans apply to classic boxing matches or football games: "In many debates in Manila High School, Elpidio Quirino was the opponent of the late Manuel Roxas, who was then president of the Rizal Debating Society in the same school."

It does no harm for an aspiring politician if he can spout his own poetry from the rostrum, preferably in his vernacular tongue, to stir the passions of the groundlings. The ability to sing is also appreciated, and a duet from the rostrum ends many a political meeting. The key word for success in

Philippine politics is "charisma." "Charisma" is used so often in the press and in political conversation that the outside visitor often leaves the islands vowing never to use the word again.

What may be called "the era of politics"—from 1957 to 1972—was dominated by two political figures, neither of whom happened to be the President of the Republic. They were Senators Diosdado Macapagal and Ferdinand Marcos.

One of the chores for anyone studying Philippine history is having to learn to say Diosdado Macapagal, and there are no short cuts. Diosdado means "God-given." The fact that it was shortened by his friends and family to "Dadong" helps a little, but not much. Macapagal once asked an American journalist how his own image could be helped in the United States, and was told, "Change your name. No American can pronounce it."

"But Filipinos can," Macapagal replied. "And they vote."

A successful lawyer and an astute politician, Macapagal, helped by a forceful wife, had been rising quietly but steadily through the political machine. He was aware that his personality lacked the charisma—sorry, flamboyance—the Philippine electors favored, and instead he concentrated on two other factors comparatively rare in high-level Philippine politics—his early poverty and his unshakable honesty.

He was born in a nipa hut in a poor *barrio* in Pampanga, north of Manila, educated himself, and passed the bar exams with one of the highest percentages in Philippine history. He made no claim for heroics during the war, but not even the most venomous of his political enemies could find any evidence of collaboration with the Japanese. His wife died of malnutrition, and he later remarried. His second wife was the former beauty queen.

War records apart, his career seemed oddly to match that of Ferdinand Marcos: both winners of the bar exam by record percentages; both elected against odds in 1949; both survivors of the 1953 debacle which decimated the Liberal Party; both married to beauty queens; both aspiring to the presidency. They were even similar in appearance. It was in approach that they were so different—Marcos always something of the soldier, flamboyant, *tout feu et toute flamme* (all fire and all flame); Macapagal the anti-soldier, quiet, thoughtful, thinking out every word before he uttered it. Marcos was the sportsman, golfer, and womanizer; Macapagal the scholar, the family man, and ascetic (he was a vegetarian).

Macapagal was, above all, a solitary man. He would invite advice and suggestions, and then, at night, sit in a chair and turn it all over in his mind, reminding one of the poet Longfellow:

> *The heights by great men reached and kept*
> *Were not attained by sudden flight,*
> *But they, while their companions slept,*
> *Were toiling upward in the night.*

Macapagal and Marcos each recognized the other as his principal adversary, and their relations varied between uneasy truce and flaming hostility.

President Garcia's period of dominance did not even last through his presidency. The elections that immediately followed Magsaysay's death were a setback for Garcia and a boost for Macapagal, thanks to a voting oddity unique even in the often eccentric politics of the Philippines.

The election matched Garcia, as incumbent President, with his running mate José Laurel, Jr. (son of the wartime President), against a Liberal ticket consisting of Chief Justice José Yulo and Diosdado Macapagal. As explained earlier, in the Philippines the presidential and vice-presidential candidates do not run in tandem. The extraordinary vote was:

Macapagal: Lib. v.p.	2,189,197
Garcia: Nac. pres.	2,072,257
Laurel: Nac. v.p.	1,783,012
Yulo: Lib. pres.	1,386,829

The best equivalent would have been if Spiro Agnew had emerged at the top of the poll in the 1972 American presidential elections, and George McGovern had come in second, with Sargent Shriver third, and Richard Nixon fourth.

The upshot was that Garcia, although elected President, was crushed, Marcos was furious, and Macapagal embarrassed but elated. Although a tough four years lay ahead of him as Vice-President under a hostile President, his unexpected triumph made him the front runner for the 1961 elections, a position which Marcos had long ago decided belonged to him.

Shunned by the President, denied access to Cabinet meetings, Macapagal had all the time he wanted to build up his strength in the countryside. He made speeches, pointing out that if the Philippine electorate so desired they could elect the first really poor man to the presidency and break the reign of the *ilustrados*. What had that reign brought them, he asked rhetorically? The bondage in which the Filipino tenant-farmer was compelled to live was worse than the peonage of Mexico. Nor could the Philippine people make scapegoats out of others—the Spaniards, the Americans, or the Japanese—as they had done in the past. The foreign devils had gone, but the native tyrants remained and, as was agonizingly obvious here as throughout history, there is no tyranny like the tyranny of one's own. To the very old, the days of the Spaniards seemed a golden age in comparison.

When Macapagal protested to the *cacique* landlords, they replied with the classic argument of the paternalist everywhere: "The peasants live in security from the cradle to the grave," they said. "Ill, they come to us for medicine. Bearing children, they ask us to be their godfather, so that they can call us compadre. Die, we bury them. What would you have? A bank to which they would have to go for loans, and a faceless bank clerk to hand them money, or tell them no? A bank in which the Government has somehow forgotten to put the allocated money in the first place? This is not Switzerland. It is not Sweden. It is the Philippines."

Its vitals gnawed at by a hostile Vice-President, the castrated presidency of Carlos Garcia stumbled on, and when the time came for the electioneering to begin for the 1961 election, Macapagal and Marcos met to agree on what should be done for the job they both wanted and which was clearly ripe to drop into the lap of whichever of the two was nominated by the party. Although Marcos was the more compelling figure, Macapagal, as Vice-President, held the better cards. The result was compromise. Macapagal would run for President, but for one term only. At the end of four years he would cede his place to Marcos. On this understanding the men agreed to campaign together.

Macapagal defeated Garcia with predictable ease, and became President. He knew the stables he had taken over were Augean, but the condition of the country was almost symbolized by the condition of Malacañang Palace when he and Evangelina Macapagal took up residence.

Every occupant of a presidential palace leaves his, or her mark, and the previous occupants of Malacañang were no exception. There were even traces of machine-gun holes left by the Japanese. But the mark left by the Garcia administration was truly disgraceful. Most of the palace grounds had been open to the public, who had been allowed to become a rabble and turn the lawns into a kind of Coney Island fairground. Cars were parked indiscriminately, and the grass had been trampled into brown dust and mud. There were soft-drink stalls, hamburger stands, and one sordid restaurant.

The palace view of the Pasig River was concealed by washing, hanging up in lines, or laid on the grass by the side of the river. The reference to Augean stables was literally apt. More than two thousand sacks of fertilizer lay rotting in sheds, delivered by some politically interested manufacturer to some politically disinterested presidential adviser. The stench was overpowering.

The situation inside the palace was, if possible, even worse. Servants had helped themselves to the silver and the china, and had stripped the residence of everything movable, down to toothpaste and toilet paper. Every evening the servants went home carrying cases and even crates of goods belonging to the palace. The carpets were filthy, and there was dust everywhere.

The task that faced Macapagal in the nation was not dissimilar to that which faced his wife in the palace, and he set about his task conscientiously. The principal problem was the problem that had faced every governor and president for the past three hundred years—land reform. He also vowed with great sincerity to put an end to graft and corruption, presenting his own example of personal honesty as that which should be followed by his countrymen. He also resolved to end smuggling, the biggest industry in the seven thousand islands. He promised to break the power of the families who dominated the nation's wealth, and dictated how the national budget should be spent. His other aim was to put an end to the influence wielded in government circles by several unsavory business operators, both Filipino and American, who had been milking the Philippines ever since the war.

It was all in vain. Beautiful, unimpeachable acts went on to the statute books, but the Congress never got around to allocating the funds to implement them. In Macapagal's four determined years of presidency, almost the only event of historical importance was the death of Emilio Aguinaldo in 1964, aged ninety-four.

The 1965 elections impending, the impatient Marcos asked Macapagal about his promise not to run for a second term and when he learned, to his great anger, that Macapagal intended to seek re-election, broke with the Liberal Party, just as Magsaysay had done, and became the standard bearer of the Nacionalistas. The battle that had been brewing for nearly twenty years between the two giant Ms of the Philippines was finally joined.

The campaign was one of the most vicious in Philippine history. Every personal slander that could be dreamed up was proffered as truth. Summonses for libel and slander flew back and forth. Violence flared in the *barrios*. Marcos's prewar conviction on the murder charge was natural ammunition, and so was his early record as a girl chaser. Macapagal's war record, or lack of it, suddenly became popular meat for the Nacionalistas. Both wives were submitted to the most astounding insults and innuendoes—nude dancing to name just one. The media wallowed in every indiscretion, and every alleged conspiracy. Snapping about the heels of the two major parties were radical groups who added to the chaos. The Huks had re-surfaced in a half-hearted way. The Moslems of Mindanao caused trouble. The "51st State" movement, which claimed to have 7 million members, campaigned to have the Philippines incorporated into the United States.

Politicians carrying guns, and often surrounded by private troops, expressed their views in the *barrios*. At quieter mo-

ments in the campaign, Macapagal recited his poems, and
Marcos and his wife, Imelda, sang duets. By the end of the
election, an estimated two hundred political murders had
been committed. Ferdinand Marcos won. He was President
at last. Macapagal departed in bitterness, not at all a good
sport about it. The curse of Malacañang Palace still held.
Not one president in history had been elected for a second
term.

Detached observers noted several facts about the election.
It might have gone much closer, or even ended in victory
for Macapagal, had it not been for the decisive influence of
Imelda Marcos, whose beauty and charm dazzled the people
in the remote villages. Macapagal's wife, Evangelina, although a good politician in her own right, was an older
woman, and no match for Imelda's sensational talents. The
observers were also agreed that now Marcos had attained
the presidency he would not yield it without a fight.

Hopes were high at first. Macapagal had done his best but
failed, the voters said. But Macapagal did not have Ferdinand's drive or his searing ambitions for greatness. Ferdinand would carry the clout to push the reforms through,
they said. Ferdinand would show 'em.

Like Macapagal, and all presidents before, Marcos promised land reform, and the elimination of graft and corruption, and an end to smuggling. In other words, even from
the start there was an air of *déja vu*. The same unbudgeable
obstacles remained. Four hundred families controlled 90
percent of the nation's wealth, dominated sugar, banking,
property ownership, manufacturing, trade. Unemployment

stood at 25 percent. Of a million diploma-holding graduates, only 600,000 were employed. The population had swelled to 38 million, and within a decade would pass that of Britain or France.

Marcos, like Macapagal, did his best. Although he did not achieve much, his personality and that of Imelda carried him through his first four years. In 1969, his opponent was Sergio Osmeña, Jr., son of the late President, a maverick and an eccentric of great charm, whose mastery of ping pong, however, was not enough to merit the presidency even for the impressionable Filipinos. Marcos became the first President to be elected to a second term, and by a record majority of 2 million votes.

This time, disillusion was immediate. Such a development was inevitable. As one critic said of the presidents of the Philippines, "You are given four years to start and finish a task which has taken other nations a generation. If you fail, we will repudiate you and every little thing you have done. And we will elect somebody else to start all over again."

Critics complained that Marcos's high spending had emptied the treasury. He was accused of personal corruption, and asked to explain the matter of 10 million dollars he had transferred from the Armed Forces to his own office for unspecified "intelligence" reasons. He was accused of bestowing political and financial favors on his wife's family, and of becoming "the richest man in Asia."

Moro wars erupted again in Mindanao. Christian families seeking virgin lands were cut down by Moslem gunfire. The 3 million Moslems were poorly led but they were des-

perate men, and much more warlike, and they feared to
suffer the fate of the American Indians. Christian vigilante
groups calling themselves *ilagas* (rats) harassed them with
armed raids. Moslem "barracudas," wearing a uniform of
black shirts, organized themselves into retaliatory gangs. The
Philippine Army was called in, and more blood, mostly
Moslem blood, was shed.

Little was done about land reform except talk. The crime
rate went on rising spectacularly, and Manila became more
notorious than New York for muggings and drug pushing,
driving tourists away and leaving the luxury hotels half
empty. Several mayors of the big cities were accused of hiring
gangs to murder drug pushers, doing more harm than good,
because it alarmed the pushers into organizing themselves in
gangs more lethal still.

From top to bottom, government departments were open
to influence peddling, graft, and payola. Government officials with modest incomes were mysteriously able to buy
automobiles and luxury homes. The size and immobility
of the government, with all its entrenched bureaucrats, left
the country like an automobile trying to go fast with its
handbrake on, so that a reformer, even granted the power,
would find his purpose revolving in an orrery of official
bodies until it burned itself out.

The bureaucrats were so much the masters of the cover-up,
the buck-pass, and the "Who? *Me?*" and had so successfully
managed to disperse their responsibilities, that even the most
pitiless torrent of reform, if it descended on them at all, fell
in a gentle and harmless spray.

The country was hectic from a virus of years of unrealized hopes and unacknowledged achievements, a condition made worse rather than better by its brilliant, strident, and frequently unscrupulous press. The Philippine press was one of the more curious marvels of world communication. It consisted of six English-language newspapers, two Spanish, and one Tagalog. Not even the British press was freer than the Philippine press. Not even the American Hearst press was more strident. Not even the Soviet press was more inaccurate. Futile to ask of such a press so enormous a sacrifice as a little reticence sometimes, futile to whisper "hush." The press was the dread tribunal of the nation's conscience, and the conscience being thus arraigned, and slightly uneasy to begin with, the verdict could be none other than an ear-splitting "Guilty!"

Despite the wit and urbanity of many of the columnists, the Philippine press had sunk hopelessly into what the Germans call *"Die Wissenschaft des nicht Wissenwerten,"* meaning "the science of what is not worth knowing."

As Ferdinand Marcos was prevented by law from running for a third term, his voice was lost in the uproar of political in-fighting by the politicians seeking the presidency in 1973. Either Marcos was ignored, or his statements met with howls of abuse and derision by the media. The taunts and the insults would have been galling to any man, not to mention a man of Marcos's pride. And Marcos offended people's feelings. One of the national characteristics of the Filipino is an Oriental deference to the outer forms of modesty. To the Occidental it is a charming but disconcerting custom, involving polite protestations of unworthiness. Somehow this trait had never touched Marcos, and his personal arrogance intensified the antagonism he engendered. Imelda Marcos could only partially check her husband's catastrophic slide. She was still popular in the *barrios,* where she shone with a luster rather like that of Eva Perón in Argentina, but Manila was the place that mattered, and every knife in the political salons was settled deeply in her back.

Only a few glimpses of hope could be found. One was in the longing of the entire people for a little peace, a little respite from the noise of politics in the press and the crime in the streets. Another was in the impeccable behavior of the Philippine Army. Had this been Latin America, or Africa, the colonels would have taken over years before. But the Philippine Army, and even the most rambunctious of its colonels, automatically respected civilian authority.

Neither the lessons of the past nor the prospects for the future induced any feelings of optimism in the Philippine breast. As the French say, *Plus ça change, plus ça reste la même chose.*

Until the year 1972 arrived . . .

Chapter 14

WHEN THE DEMOCRACY STOPPED

IT IS AN oddity of nature that national disasters, both God-made and man-made, tend to divide into urban and rural, affecting one without touching the other. In Ireland, for example, bombs, mayhem and, historically, starvation and oppression, occur "elsewhere" while leaving the gracious life of Dublin untouched. In some countries, like France, and to a lesser extent, Italy, the capitals catch the blast while the rest of the country continues as if nothing has happened. In the Soviet Union, the authorities make certain that whatever disasters occur anywhere in the land, no echo is allowed to reach the ears of Moscow.

The Philippines is not like that. Disaster strikes everywhere. When a volcano erupts, Manila trembles. When there are floods, Manila's drains—built by the Spaniards—regurgitate on the city, leaving whole areas under water and leading to such quaint sights as, for example, a barber going about his business, shaving and cutting hair, up to his waist in water.

In the summer of 1972, one did not have to leave Manila to realize that some major catastrophe had occurred. The city sagged under the rains and storms until the city administration seemed almost threatened with collapse. The Philippines is storm country, and is hit by an average of fifty-seven typhoons a year. The summer of 1972 marked the worst storm in Philippine history, when Luzon was devastated. Not one but two monsoons passed over the area in quick succession, turned around, came back, and stayed, blowing themselves to bits over the island.

All the summer crop of rice, sugar, fruits, and vegetables was destroyed. Livestock and poultry were drowned, and roads, gaspipes and waterpipes, dams, bridges and railways, factories, warehouses, and fishponds were all swept away. Literally hundreds of thousands of people lived in trees for up to thirty days until they were rescued by helicopters, many of the helicopters supplied by U.S. Navy relief teams. The waters poured unchecked and unabated through entire provinces because loggers had been illegally chopping down trees to sell to Japan.

At the same time large areas of Mindanao and the Visayas were gasping from a record drought, and praying for rain.

The task of recovery was almost too staggering to contemplate. Think of the effort required to remove three feet of packed sand from an acre of farmland, and then think of thousands and thousands of hectares of the country's richest farmland all similarly inundated, a desert for as far as you could see from a helicopter or even an airplane. The damage was conservatively estimated at 225 million dollars. To restore the basic communications alone cost the government 55 million dollars.

Financial aid was forthcoming through the pipeline of a consortium headed by the United States and Japan. But when President Marcos presented the sums to Congress, he was met by objections that were familiar to political ears. Certain congressmen insisted on bigger cuts for their own areas, and also that the funds should be allocated in the congressmen's own names. Corruption was not waiting for the apple to fall before biting it.

To make the situation all the more heartbreaking, the disaster occurred just as the economy was beginning to show some glimmers of light. The graphs were marking a cautious upswing. The floods washed all that away and rendered the graphs meaningless. The Philippines had been set back an estimated five years, during which time the population would grow by more than 5 million people, more than nullifying what gains might be made.

All the time, three wars were being waged, one between the Christians and Moslems in Mindanao, one in Luzon where a Maoist offshoot of the Huks showed dangerous signs of cohesion, and a third in the streets against the drug pushers and the organized gangs. Throughout the traditionally pro-American country, a new unpleasant Marxist movement denounced American imperialism, and if it made little impact on the people, who had other things to worry about, it inhibited American investors from putting money into the economy.

Altogether, the Philippines was too sodden and tired to be compared to a tinderbox, and when the match was struck and martial law declared, it seemed to make not so much an explosion as a "phut." Ferdinand Marcos had been expected by the weary country to declare martial law for years, or if he did not, to groom Imelda Marcos for the presidency in 1973. A commission had been at work for months on a political reform project that would turn the Philippines from a presidential form of democracy in the American fashion to a British-style Parliamentary democracy. There was nothing revolutionary in such a move. Parliamentary democracy suits the Asian political temperament. It had worked for a quarter of a century in India. It was practiced in Ceylon, and it had been adopted by the new nation of Bangladesh.

On the night of September 23, 1972, while the newspapers of Manila were preparing for their daily shriek, police walked into the offices and the broadcasting stations, ordered the staff to go home, and posted announcements that the buildings were sealed and under military control. Domestic airlines were grounded, and overseas telephone operators refused to accept incoming calls. University campuses were closed.

Editors and opposition politicians were imprisoned but not otherwise ill treated, and most were released in ones and twos. In the cities a curfew was declared from midnight to 4 A.M. (many Filipinos rise at that hour to beat the heat).

Marcos ordered all private guns to be handed in, and the

mountains of arms accumulated in the police stations. At the same time, major drug pushers were arrested, tried, convicted, and promptly shot in public. The streets of the cities became notably safer.

Nobody took to the hills. But Imelda Marcos, in front of the television screen, was attacked by a madman who slashed away at her flailing arms before being shot dead. She was not seriously wounded, but the incident was a horrible and terrifying one, and demonstrated the fragility of Philippine life.

In this manner, democracy died in the Philippines after a long and noble struggle against overwhelming odds. It had shown much promise and produced many fine democrats.

Educated Filipinos, most of them willing to give the experiment a chance, would have been more optimistic if the circumstances had been different; if Ferdinand Marcos throughout his single-minded career had not made his ruthlessness and personal ambition quite so visible; if Imelda Marcos had not been such a compelling force; if Marcos had issued the decree from a position of strength, and not when his second administration was in tatters; if Marcos had not been so near to compulsory retirement from office. If . . . if . . . if. . . .

If the perennial cancers of Philippine life—land exploitation, corruption, crime, excessive population increase—could be eradicated by strong one-man government, then the future course of the Philippines would turn it into a power quite different from anything it had been before. For better or for worse. Any man who assumes dictatorial power must

contemplate the maxim, "He who lives by the sword. . . ."
Knives both political and physical—shafts of wit from
Forbes Park, and bolo knives from the *barrios*—are rarely
hidden very deeply in Philippine society. The place of Ferdinand Marcos in his nation's history depends absolutely on
how long he lives.

The presidential palace of Malacañang is a delicate white
Spanish colonial mansion standing on the south bank of the
Pasig River. It was built as a private home in 1802 by one
Don Luis Rocha, who sold it to a friend, Don José Miguel
Fomento, a colonel in the Spanish Army. When Fomento
died, his relatives in Spain decided it was too distant to
maintain as a residence and sold it to the Spanish administration for five thousand pesos. In order to pay for it, the
Spanish prudently put a six-peso head tax on every Chinese
living in the country. It was first used only as a summer
residence, but when the Palace of Intramuros was destroyed
by an earthquake in 1863, it became the permanent residence
of the Governor General.

The residential quarters at Malacañang are on the second
floor, above a high-ceilinged reception hall. The hall is dominated by three magnificent crystal chandeliers, imported
from Czechoslovakia before World War II, and buried in
the grounds of the palace during the Japanese occupation.

On the walls are hung oil paintings of all the Presidents of
the Philippines, and the effect of their collective gaze is
enough to induce humility in even the most arrogant. What
makes them so impressive is their *immediacy*. They are all

modern. There are no wigs, no ruffles, no Victorian beards or fobs to lend distance to their regard, no Lincolns, Bonapartes, or Bismarcks to offer a definable schoolboy's-eye view of history. These Presidents, every one of them, are all men of our time, and they gaze from their paintings like people one knows, a jury of peers deciding the verdict of history on any who would join their august ranks. Even General Emilio Aguinaldo, the first President, back in 1898, is a contemporary, remaining an ornament of the Philippine scene until his death in 1964. The painting of Aguinaldo shows him as a young man in uniform, with Oriental features and the famous, curious brush haircut that makes the top of his head look flat.

One then regards the painting of Manuel Quezon, father of the modern Philippines, President of the Commonwealth, and almost unchallenged ruler of the country from 1922 until his death in exile in 1944. He is as handsome as a Roman god, and his languidly held cigarette only emphasizes his hauteur. He is immaculately dressed, with a carnation in his buttonhole, and a silk foulard handkerchief in his breast pocket. His jaw is ruthless, and his mouth is downturned distastefully at the corners, as though he is expecting his intelligence to be insulted. One would dread to arouse the wrath of *that* man.

Next to President Quezon hangs the portrait of Elpidio Quirino, President from 1948 to 1953. Here is a Spanish–Philippine aristocrat, and a man of the world, with a celebrated sense of humor, and a lack of interest in the company of fools. He was, in fact, playing his own private, sophisticated joke on society, beçause this apparent embodiment of the voluptuary and sensualist wore a hair shirt of unremitting grief.

One turns to Manuel Roxas, President for only two years, from 1946 to his death, of a stroke, in 1948, another aristocrat from the province of Capiz, lean, brilliant, vulpine, so poised and so tautly sprung one feels that if one blinked an eye he would be gone. He was a hero in his own time, and yet he died before his full service could be rendered to his country; this is the curse of the Philippines.

The same applies to Ramon Magsaysay, killed in an air crash in 1957, a "hero of democracy" in American philately. In the painting he is very much the tough guy, his muscles almost bursting from his biceps, his knuckles gnarled. Here is a man who can love a woman, or sock a man on the jaw. He probably chews glass for amusement.

The difference between Magsaysay and José Laurel is almost symbolized by the clothes they are wearing. Magsaysay is wearing the *barong tagalog,* as he always did in life. Laurel is in white tie and tails, his jacket slightly too big for a frame diminished by the malnutrition of wartime, and emphasizing his smallness. His face is kindly, sympathetic, highly intelligent. He assumed the fearful burden of the presidency of the Republic that was created by the Japanese Army during the occupation. Although it involved collaboration with a brutal oppressor, it carried almost no taint of Pétainism, and Laurel proved that he continued to enjoy the love and esteem of the Philippine people by coming within a whisker of winning the presidency of the new Republic in 1949. His is the face of a good man who has no apologies to make to history.

President Sergio Osmeña, who waited for the presidency for ten years under Quezon, and then enjoyed it for only two, from 1944 to 1946, looks you in the eye with confidence and urbanity, handsome even in old age, a scholar elegantly dressed in a suit that was probably made in London. In his brief term as President he was able to demonstrate the maturity of Philippine democracy under stresses that would have reduced most countries to anarchism, revolution, or Communism. He conceded the 1946 election to General Roxas with a grace rarely equaled even in the most experienced democracies and retired to his home in Cebu to spend the rest of his life reading and praying; his serenity of spirit requiring no prop this side of the grave, he disdained even the luxury of autobiography.

President Carlos Garcia (1957–1961) has been hung in a corner. A Filipino Laniel, or Bidault, a war hero when he was fifty years old, but proving, like Laniel and Bidault, that heroic exaltation in war is not necessarily a qualification for the highest political office, and unlike many men unexpectedly called to power, he failed to rise to the office. He regards one smoothly, without excuses, as though his claim to immortality is so modest as to be undeserving of minute examination. "More sinned against than sinning," his defenders affirm.

Like Magsaysay, Diosdado Macapagal (1961–1965) wears the *barong tagalog,* and the painting shows off his quiet, civilized, rather old-fashioned good looks, his thick black hair parted in the middle and plastered down with cream, in the same Rudolph Valentino style he cultivated in his impoverished youth. He looks suitably ambivalent for a man unsure of the cards that he has been dealt. Small, beautiful hands are held in repose but appear capable of the most electric gestures.

The portrait of Ferdinand Marcos, even as he holds the reins of power, has about it a lean and hungry look, and such men are dangerous. His face has so much power and beauty that one longs for the suggestion of a smile, or even the gleam of humor that shows in the eyes of Macapagal, his old adversary. This is the face of a man both determined and driven, aware that his place in history will be compared with those of his peers hanging on the walls, every single one of whom he knew in life, a claim no future President of the Philippines will be able to make.

The Filipino, despite his fatalism, has a pessimistic attitude to death. The prospect does not inspire him to grandeur, as it does the Japanese. He accepts the fact that on the other side of that dread boundary he is likely to be given a pretty hard time. As José Rizal writes in *Noli Me Tangere,* "A visit to the churches and cemeteries of the Philippines on All Saints Day (which, in French, is known as the Day of the Dead) would have sufficed to convince the skeptic that this fearful frame of mind is not exceptional. The greatest optimist imagined his great-grandparents still roasting in Purgatory and, always provided that he did not end up in a worse place, expected to keep them company himself for a considerable time."

Beholding those faces every morning as he moves through the great hall to the terrace for his breakfast in the open air, Ferdinand Marcos must contemplate his place in history not only on the moanings of Filipino and American historians and liberals, not only on the silenced Manila media or the wailing of the *New York Times* editorials, but also on the eyes that gaze down on him, like the ghosts of Ruddigore, from the walls of the palace he intends to occupy for an indefinite time to come.

BIBLIOGRAPHY

Alejandrino, José: *The Price of Freedom,* Manila, 1949.

Aluit, Alfonso J.: *The Conscience of a Nation,* Manila, 1953.

Baclagon, Uldarico S.: *Philippine Campaigns,* Manila, 1952.

Bohlen, Charles E.: *Witness to History,* W. W. Norton, New York, 1973.

Buenafe, Manuel E.: *Wartime Philippines,* Manila, 1950.

Caballero, Isabelo P. and M. Grecia Conception: *Quezon,* Manila, 1935.

de la Costa, Horacio, S.J.: *Asia and the Philippines,* 1961.

Guerrero, Léon Ma.: *The First Filipino,* Manila, 1961.

Hayden, Joseph Ralston: *The Philippines, a Study in National Development,* pp 170–171. Macmillan, New York, 1942.

Keith, Agnes Newton: *White Man Returns,* Little Brown, Boston, 1950.

Laus, E. L.: *The Ten Most Outstanding Filipino National Leaders*, Manila, 1951.

Malcolm, George A.: *The First Malayan Republic*, Christopher Publishing House, Boston, 1951.

Palma, Dr. Rafael: *Pride of the Malay Race*, Manila, 1949.

Quezon, Manuel L.: *The Good Fight*, Appleton Century, New York, 1946.

Quirino, Carlos: *Magsaysay of the Philippines*, Manila, 1958.

——: *The Young Aguinaldo*, Manila, 1969.

——: *Quezon, Man of Destiny*, McCullough Printing Company, New York, 1935.

Ravenholt, Albert: *The Philippines*, Van Nostrand, Princeton, 1962.

Recto, Claro: *Three Years of Enemy Occupation*, Manila, 1949.

Retizos, Isidro L. and D. H. Soriano: *Philippines Who's Who*, Manila, 1970.

Rizal, Dr. José: *Noli Me Tangere*, Madrid, 1887 (translation by Léon Ma. Guerrero, Longmans, London 1961).

——: *El Filibusterismo*, 1889 (translation by Léon Ma. Guerrero, Longmans, London, 1961).

Romulo, General Carlos P.: *I Saw the Fall of the Philippines*, Doubleday, New York, 1942.

——: *I Walked With Heroes*, Holt, Rinehart and Winston, New York, 1961.

Romulo, General Carlos P. and Marvin Gray: *The Magsaysay Story*, John Day, New York, 1956.

Smith, Robert Aura: *Philippine Freedom 1946–1958*, Columbia University Press, New York, 1958.

Spence, Harzell: *For Every Tear a Victory* (authorized biography of Ferdinand Marcos), McGraw Hill, New York, 1964.

INDEX

177

ABOUT THE AUTHOR

GEOFFREY BOCCA was born in the north of England and has had a varied career, starting as an office boy when he was 15, and including service as a paratrooper in World War II, when he was taken prisoner and escaped.

At the age of 20 he became the youngest war correspondent in Europe, working for the *London Daily Express*. He emigrated to the United States and, at 23, was chief New York correspondent of the Kemsley (now Thomson) Newspapers of London.

As a foreign correspondent he covered many historical events, witnessing, uninvited, Castro's execution squads in the Cabana Prison of Havana.

Mr. Bocca first went to the Philippines in 1965 with Quentin Reynolds to write a profile of President Macapagal. Mr. Reynolds died suddenly, but Mr. Bocca stayed on to study what he considered the most fascinating and appealing people he had ever met, and became an authority on the country's history and politics, a deep sympathizer of its human problems, and a friend of many of its leading figures.

The author has written many articles, books of biography, history, travel, true-crime, and so on. He maintains three homes—one in the United States, one in London, and one on the French Riviera, and continues his world travels.